PRACTICAL
jewellery making techniques:
problem solving

STEPHEN O'KEEFFE

A & C BLACK • LONDON

First published in Great Britain 2011
A&C Black Publishers
36 Soho Square
London W1D 3QY
www.acblack.com

ISBN: 978-14081-0581-8

Copyright © 2011 Stephen O'Keeffe

A CIP catalogue record for this book is available from the British Library

Stephen O'Keeffe has asserted his rights under the Copyright, Design and Patents Act, 1988, to be identified as the author of this work.

Cover design: Sutchinda Rangsi Thompson
Page design: Susan McIntyre
Commissioning editor: Susan James
Managing editor: Davida Saunders
Copy editor: Julian Beecroft
Proofreader: Julie Brooke

Typeset in: 11 on 14.5pt Celeste

This book is produced using paper that is made from wood grown in managed, sustainable forests. It is natural, renewable and recyclable. The logging and manufacturing processes conform to the environmental regulations of the country of origin.

Printed and bound in China

PRACTICAL
jewellery making techniques:
problem solving

Contents

Introduction

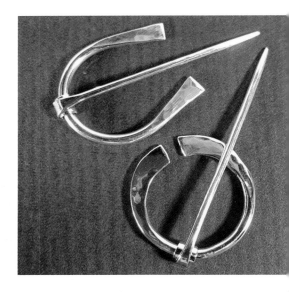

THE SKILLS USED BY THE WORKER IN PRECIOUS METALS are difficult to master without years of training and practice. Much of the work carries risks, and disaster is only moments away. Many books on jewellery-making, perhaps written by professional silversmiths, appear to assume a level of skill on the part of their readers that is quite unrealistic. When you have carried out a process a thousand times it must be difficult to see how hard it is for someone doing it for the first time. The teacher sees these difficulties countless times.

Being a teacher, rather than a craftsman, I have written this book as a guide informed by the many difficulties encountered – both my own and those of my students – during years of grappling with the demands of this fascinating and often challenging craft. The book is an attempt to show how the aspiring jewellery maker – not necessarily the beginner, but certainly the non-professional – can make successful pieces without needing to expend an unreasonable amount of time and effort. Perhaps an alternative title for the book could be 'Jewellery-making for Amateurs'.

We should not expect to gain success too easily; these are not projects with the skills taken out. Nor is this book an idiot's guide to jewellery-making. We should not underestimate the difficulties of the work, and neither should we seek to remove them altogether, even if this were possible. The satisfaction gained from creating jewellery will be all the greater for overcoming problems along the way.

Jewellery-making is an ancient craft, rich in tradition, and many of the tools used have changed little since the earliest times. It is well that we keep in mind the craftsmen of the past, for an appreciation of their work and some understanding of how it was made enhances the enjoyment and satisfaction we derive from our own work. Such knowledge also helps us to keep our own modest achievements in perspective. Learning from the past and making use of traditional tools and techniques is still, and will always be, a significant part of jewellery-making.

I make my own silver solder using tiny offcuts of silver. I have a ready supply of brass and copper wire an accurate balance with which to weigh it, and also a rolling mill to reduce the alloy to the required thickness. I do this by choice. I could easily buy my solder but I gain greater satisfaction from jewellery-making by using homemade solder. In the 19th century, the Native American craftsmen of the Southwest United States would have melted a spent cartridge case and a silver dollar in a charcoal fire using bellows, and beaten the resulting mixture into a usable form on a piece of iron rail. He would, of course, have done this out of necessity. As you gain experience of jewellery-making you will find that your respect for these craftsmen of old increases.

Most jewellery-making projects have a particularly difficult and often risky stage where disaster is likely to strike. The jewellery maker does not exist who has not at some stage melted his work at a crucial stage, or tangled his nearly finished work in a polishing machine. Identifying these stages, and suggesting ways of limiting any difficulties and hopefully of overcoming them, makes up a large part of this book. For every stumbling block there may be a strategy for dealing with it, or perhaps an alternative course of action. Traditional techniques can be made more accessible with some slight modification. The aim is to provide the student of jewellery-making with a realistic and achievable path to success.

When confronted with a problem it is often better to stand back from it and think. There may be an alternative approach, perhaps more than one, which is better suited to the situation. This may take a little longer, but the race is not always to the swift. Many of the strategies suggested here use simple tools, devices or jigs, often made from readily available items such as nails, paperclips or screws, which will enable the difficulties to be more easily overcome. These devices may also make the production of future projects easier, as they prove their worth time after time. They may also provide a necessary uniformity in units such as links in a chain, or pairs of earrings. Other strategies are tips born out of practical experience, and some lateral thinking, to enable some of the more difficult processes to be carried out with less risk.

Teaching is a collaborative process, and all teachers owe a debt of gratitude to those they teach. In my case this debt is greater than most. The struggles of my students have inspired much of the content of this book, and many of the strategies have been developed in response to their needs. My classes have often proved a valuable testing ground for my projects and ideas. I am particularly fortunate to have taught so many articulate and intelligent students, whose feedback has been invaluable.

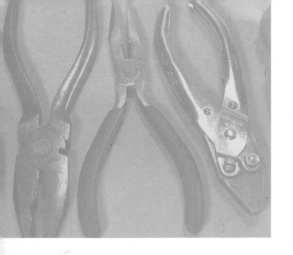

1 Tools for the jewellery maker

A GLANCE THROUGH THE CATALOGUE OF A SILVERSMITH'S suppliers will reveal a bewildering array of tools and equipment. It would be very easy to spend a small fortune on equipping a workshop, and it could be said that a jewellery maker and his money are soon parted.

There are times when there is no alternative to buying the best-quality tools, the cheaper ones being a false economy. One of the joys of creative work is in using fine-quality tools, which can often make light of the task in hand. However, finances usually dictate that such pleasures are better kept to a minimum, or at least indulged with discretion.

There is often a viable alternative to acquiring some of the more expensive tools, and, moreover, the creative process can be made more satisfying by the use of homemade tools, or those which have been adapted from some other purpose. Tools designed for jewellery-making are often more expensive than general-purpose ones. Since the latter can be put to use in other ways, this will inevitably make them even better value.

If the opportunity should arise to acquire second-hand tools this should be taken advantage of. Many old tools are better-made than their modern equivalents, and there is a pleasure to be gained from working with tools used by craftsmen of a previous age. Although this section is written with an eye to those on a budget, those who can afford it may ignore the advice offered and indulge themselves – it won't be difficult.

Older tools are often more affordable and of better quality than modern ones.

THE WORKBENCH

The first requirement in a workshop is a table or bench, and the most important characteristic of this table or bench is that it should be solid. It is virtually impossible to carry out the hammering processes involved in jewellery-making on a surface that shakes and trembles under the hammer. A shelf just beneath the tabletop is useful for housing tools not in immediate use, and will also add stability to the table. Two little screws or hooks are needed on the front of this shelf. Use these to hang the corners of an apron for catching small parts and scraps of metal that would otherwise fall on the floor.

Most jewellery-making is carried out at eye level, often with the use of a magnifying glass. If you want to avoid the discomfort of constantly bending over the bench, then the bench top must be higher than that of most other work surfaces. Putting blocks under the legs may be necessary, but if this is not an option then sitting on a lower stool is a less satisfactory alternative.

The bench peg on which much of the sawing, filing and other work is done should be detachable. It is sometimes convenient to be able to work in the middle of the bench, with your chest pressed against its edge. To enable this, hold the bench peg in place with a G-clamp or, if making a hole in the bench is not a problem, with a nut and bolt. The bench peg can also be used, with the addition of some simple extras, as a holding device (see pp.42–3).

A detachable bench peg is useful for many jewellery-making tasks.

A selection of tools for marking out and measuring. FROM LEFT TO RIGHT **Tape measure, try square, permanent pen, clutch pencil scriber, dividers, centre punch, dividers, metal ruler, plastic ruler.**

MARKING-OUT TOOLS

For marking out and measuring, a 150 mm (6 in.) ruler is long enough for most purposes. These are usually made of steel, but a plastic one is cheaper with the advantage that it won't scratch highly polished metal. Carefully saw off the end to make it exactly zero, which is the way a steel rule is made. Whenever you need to make a longer measurement, you'll find a flexible tape is more convenient than a longer rigid rule.

Most marking out on polished metal can be done with a fine permanent pen. This will not scratch the metal and the marks can easily be removed with a spirit such as nail varnish remover. 'Permanent' means that

the mark is unlikely to rub off by accident. The line made by a fine-line pen is not always accurate enough, so when a more precise line is required a scriber is used. These are usually made of thin steel, and being so thin they are not very comfortable in the hand. A clutch pencil with the point from a pair of dividers, as used by draughtsmen, makes a better scriber, and the dividers themselves make a good substitute for the more expensive kind of dividers used by silversmiths. Dividers are used for scribing arcs, for scribing a line parallel to an edge and for marking the centres of a line of holes equidistant to one another.

The fine line made by these instruments can be difficult to see on polished metal, so the surface can first be shaded with the permanent pen, so that the line shows more clearly. When dividers are used to scribe an arc, the stationary point must lodge in a small indent made with a centre punch. This punch, which is ground to an angle of 90 degrees, is also used to mark the centre of where a hole is to be drilled.

The templates used by draughtsmen for creating ellipses and circles are useful, as these are common shapes in jewellery-making. A try square is used to check whether an angle is 90 degrees, and also with a scriber or permanent pen to make a line square to an edge.

HOLDING TOOLS

Whatever the process being carried out, it is essential that the work is firmly held. Jewellery is very often small and difficult to hold securely. Sometimes considerable force must be applied to it, demanding a firm grip. A device that holds the work securely and with very little effort by the user can be invaluable. When accidents happen it is often the hand holding the piece of work that suffers. If it is securely held, both hands are free to control the tool. Two hands will usually control the tool more effectively than one, and both will be behind the tool and therefore out of danger.

A small vice that can be clamped to the bench is useful; one with 5 cm (2 in.) jaws will be big enough for most purposes. The jaws on a vice are usually roughened for a better grip, but these can seriously damage the surface of the metal. Vice guards made of a soft metal such as copper must always be used unless the section of the work being held is waste, or you are holding a tool or a jig.

Several pairs of pliers are needed, the most useful of which are the parallel-jawed kind. The great advantage of the parallel action is that the jaws are in contact with work throughout its length, giving a much more secure grip than the central-pivot type. The other advantage of parallel pliers is that, having no central pivot, the work being held can pass right through the jaws and out through the handles. This makes it possible to hold, end on,

Shading the surface of polished metal with a permanent pen can make it easier to see finely scribed lines.

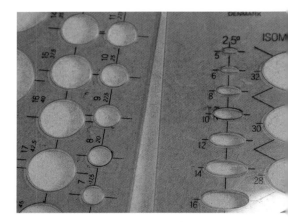

Templates can be used to create circles and ellipses.

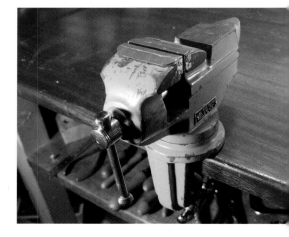

A small vice that can be fixed to the bench with a clamp will be useful.

wire and long strips of metal, which will sometimes be necessary.

Snipe-nosed pliers, the jaws of which taper down towards the tip, and a pair of round-nosed pliers will be needed. Snipe-nosed pliers can sometimes be too pointed as force applied over too small an area can mark soft metal jump rings, etc. Grind and file these down to about 3 mm wide. All of these pliers have smooth jaws, which will reduce the risk of marking soft metal. General-purpose pliers with serrated jaws can be used for jewellery-making, but the jaws must first be filed smooth.

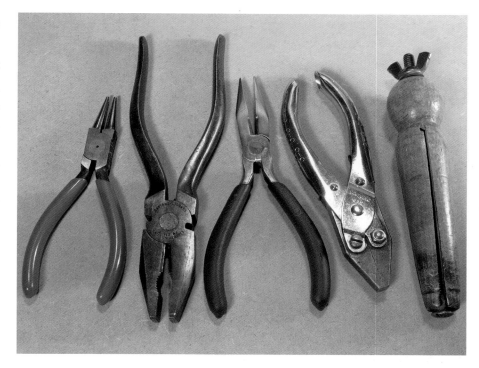

A selection of pliers. FROM LEFT TO RIGHT **Round-nosed pliers, engineer's pliers, snipe-nosed pliers, parallel pliers, ring clamp.**

Engineer's pliers, which have serrated jaws, are sometimes required if a firm grip is needed – when wire drawing, for example. These pliers have powerful wire cutters on the side, that will cut thicker wire.

Ring clamps and other holding tools made for a specific purpose are very useful, and many of them can be made in a home workshop (see p.32).

Cutting tools. FROM LEFT TO RIGHT **Shears, end cutters made from pincers, side cutters.**

CUTTING TOOLS

Cost-cutting on pliers is quite acceptable, as these tools are not subject to much wear. The same cannot be said for cutting tools. A pair of shears or cutters that will not hold an edge will be practically useless. Try to buy a recognised brand; if there isn't a name on the blade, avoid it. A pair of good-quality jeweller's shears will last for years, and will cut silver and other metals up to 1 mm (18 B&S) thick. A pair of scissors, provided they too are of good quality, will also cut sheet silver.

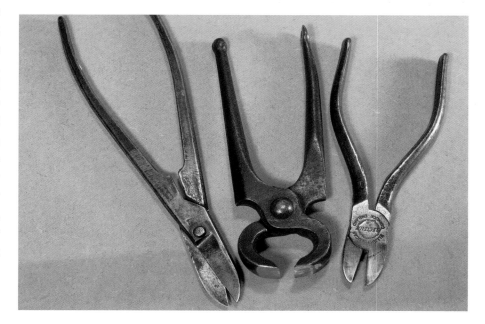

Cutters, which are used on wire, can be either end or side cutters. Side cutters are more useful, as more force can be created at the bottom of the blade, near to the pivot, when cutting thick wire. Very thick wire, more than 3 mm, is usually best sawn with a piercing saw.

An acceptable pair of end cutters can be made from a pair of pincers, the tool used by carpenters for pulling out nails. Simply grind down the ends until they are sharp. They may no longer be used on steel nails (because the sharp edge would be damaged on a nail), but a very neat cut can be made with them on silver or copper wire.

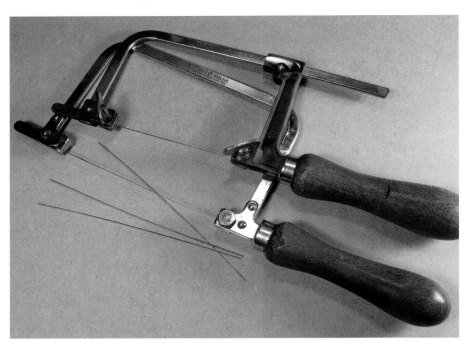

Piercing saws; adjustable (top) and non-adjustable (bottom).

The piercing-saw frame can be either plain or adjustable. The plain one only accepts whole blades; the adjustable frame can be shortened to use up broken blades, of which there will be many. The fixing at either end is tightened by a wing nut, often with pliers, as it is difficult to tighten with fingers alone. The fixings on this fixed-frame saw have been replaced with less cumbersome bolts, which can be tightened with a tube spanner. Piercing saw blades range from 4, the coarsest, down to 0/8, the finest. The best one for most purposes is 0/3, which, if used with care, will last as long as any. The piercing saw will cut steel bolts and nails very effectively, if rather slowly. An alternative for this type of work is the junior hacksaw, a general-purpose tool which will also cut wood and plastic. Lubricate the blade of the piercing saw from time to time by wiping it on a block of beeswax.

A penknife has many usees – for example, as a scraping tool, for removing burrs on the edge of a piece of metal, and for cutting wood and leather items.

Two sharpening stones, one coarse and one smooth, should be used regularly. Sharp tools are much more effective, and far safer, than blunt ones.

A penknife and Arkansas and India stones.

DRILLS

For most drilling operations an electric hand drill will serve the purpose very well. The cordless version, preferably with two batteries, will be most convenient to use. This type does not usually have a lock on the switch. Improvise with a cable tie, which can be slipped over the switch to lock it in the 'on' position, freeing both hands to keep the drill upright.

A small bench pedestal drill is useful for heavy-duty drilling, and also because it will always move up and down vertically.

Drill bits used on metal should be made of high-speed steel (HSS). Buy an extra supply of the smaller sizes, as these are more easily broken.

A cordless electric hand drill.

FILES

The jewellery maker uses a much smoother file than those used in other crafts. Two large files will satisfy most requirements, the first being a 15 cm (6 in.) smooth hand file. The hand file has a safe edge, which is completely smooth. This edge is used against a shoulder – for example, the setting for a stone – which must not be scratched.

A 10 cm (4 in.) smooth half-round file (rounded on one side and flat on the other) is used mainly for smoothing inside curves. A set of ten or twelve needle files can be useful for more intricate work. These files have sharp points which can easily break off, but will contain every shape you may need to get into awkward corners.

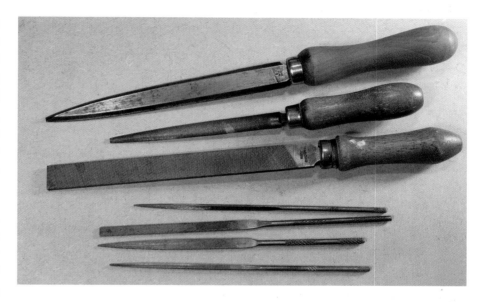

Hand files of assorted sizes, from top: Barrette file, half round file, hand file and four needle files.

Emery boards are also used for smoothing metal, and these are simple to make yourself. Three sheets of wet-and-dry emery paper (400, 600 and 800 grit) and strips of 300 x 25 x 6 mm (12 x 1 x ¼ in.) plywood with double-sided adhesive tape will make 15 boards. Wrap the emery paper around three sides of the plywood strip to leave a safe edge of plywood on the remaining edge.

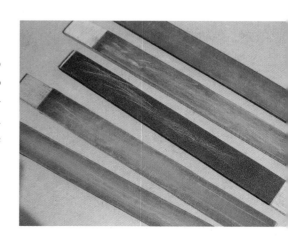

Emery boards.

FROM LEFT TO RIGHT **A heavy hammer for punches and nails, a ball-peen hammer and two cross-peen hammers.**

HAMMERS AND STAKES

Two hammers, one with a ball peen and the other with a cross peen, will be needed. Silversmiths' hammers can be expensive, but an ordinary hammer can be abraded and polished to make a perfectly good substitute. The two flat faces should be rounded off, one more so than the other. These polished hammers are used only for planishing soft metals such as silver and bronze. A third, slightly heavier, unpolished hammer will be needed for the hammering of punches and nails.

For a stake, a short length of round steel bar, 25 or 30 mm (1 or 1¹⁄₈ in.), slightly rounded on one end and flat on the other, will serve the purpose well. This is abraded and polished like the planishing hammers and held in a hole in a wooden block.

Three stakes in a wooden block.

The block should be about 100 x 100 x 50 mm (4 x 4 x 2 in.) to make a stable base. About 25 mm (1 in.) of the bar should be sticking up above the surface of the wood. If the bar is smoothed and polished on its side, as well as the ends, it will fit snugly in a hole of the same diameter. The bottom of the hole should be drilled through with a smaller drill bit to allow the stake to be pushed out from underneath in the event that it should get stuck. One block can be used to hold several stakes of different sizes, each of which are rounded on one side and flat on the other.

A mallet is required for forming metal without marking its surface. Metalworking mallets are usually made from rolled hide, which is quite heavy, making a small one very effective. A hardwood mallet is satisfactory, but must be made larger, wood being lighter than hide, and so will be more awkward to use.

SOLDERING EQUIPMENT

Most silver soldering can be done with the kind of blowtorch used in the kitchen to caramelise sugar and to skin tomatoes. The heat produced by these tools is enough to melt all grades of solder, and the flame is narrow and well-defined so it can be directed exactly as required. The gas used is lighter fuel, which is readily available and inexpensive.

Sometimes, when the work is heavy, a cook's torch will be too small to heat it up quickly enough for successful soldering. In this situation a larger torch, such as those used by plumbers, may be necessary. These have a separate gas cylinder which is discarded when empty. The flame produced is not as well-defined as that of the smaller torch, but being larger it will heat up heavier work more quickly. These torches become top-heavy when they are less than half full, so a broad base is essential.

When using a torch, protect the work bench with a piece of fireproof material. Place a sheet of plywood under it for extra protection. The scorch marks on this one (right) will testify to its usefulness. Some

A rolled hide mallet (top) and a wooden mallet (bottom).

A large blowtorch of the kind used by plumbers (LEFT), and a cook's torch for the kitchen (RIGHT).

Fireproof bricks and a piece of charcoal are essential soldering equipment.

A cone of borax is ground against a slate with water, to make flux of a thin consistency, like milk. Water is best added with a pipette. The flux is applied to the work with a paintbrush.

pieces of charcoal – barbecue fuel will do – will need to be placed around the work to reflect the heat onto it. Charcoal will continue to burn after it has been used for soldering, so you must remember to quench it after use.

Silver solder is sold in strips; two grades, hard and easy, will be sufficient for most needs. The flux used in silver soldering is borax, which can be bought in powder or liquid form and also as a solid cone. Solid borax is mixed to the right consistency by grinding the cone with water in a borax dish or on a piece of slate. A small brush is used to apply the flux to the work, and a pair of pointed tweezers to place the pieces of solder.

Two containers of water should be used, a clean one for mixing the flux, and another one for quenching the work and for rinsing it after pickling (see below) in the acid solution. A dropper or pipette, to add just the right amount of water to the flux mixture, completes the soldering equipment.

Acid pickle. Brass or copper tweezers, or a piece of copper wire, are useful for hooking pieces out of the solution when the spent flux has been dissolved.

THE ACID PICKLE

After soldering, the work must be soaked in a sulphuric-acid solution, known as pickle, to dissolve the spent flux and clean off any surface oxides. The acid pickle is mixed to about ten parts of water to one of acid. A container of heatproof glass or glazed earthenware is used, and the water is poured in first. The acid should be added to the water a little at a time, as heat is generated as they mix. **Water must NEVER be added to acid. This can cause a violent and dangerous reaction.** Only non-ferrous tongs or tweezers, such as those made of brass or copper, should be used in the acid pickle.

POLISHING EQUIPMENT

A polishing machine with several mops will save a great deal of time on the finishing stage of a project. Such machines are very dirty in use, and take up a lot of workshop space. Some kind of vacuum extraction system is essential if the entire work area is not to be covered in polishing dust. If a separate area is available for polishing, such as a garage or a shed, this may be the best option.

A less-expensive alternative to the dedicated polishing machine is to adapt an electric hand drill. Discs covered with felt or leather can be mounted on spindles and held in the chuck of the drill. Another option is strips of carpet fastened to a board. These are used with tripoli or rouge, and can be surprisingly effective.

A purpose-made electric polishing machine.

Polishing pads covered with leather, made in the same way as emery boards, are used with a succession of ever-finer polishes. The polish can be in block form or as powder made into a paste with water or oil. Old leather belts can be cut into pieces and used with polishing paste. Old toothbrushes are handy, used either with rouge or soap for the final finishing process. All these alternatives to the polishing machine will take more time, but are no less effective on the finished product.

Store all polishes and their pads and wheels in separate containers to prevent the finer polishes from being contaminated by the coarser ones. Keep a plentiful supply of polishing cloths for final polishing.

ABOVE RIGHT **Pieces of old leather belt and old toothbrushes are good for polishing.**

RIGHT **Polish comes in block or powder form and in different grades.**

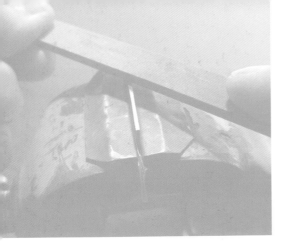

2 Basic techniques

THE TECHNIQUES OF THE JEWELLERY MAKER can be divided into four main areas.

1. Cutting and wasting (including sawing, drilling, punching, cutting with shears and filing)
2. Forming (including bending, planishing and forging)
3. Joining by soldering
4. Polishing and finishing techniques.

The techniques are explained in general terms with examples that are typical of the processes involved. Two simple projects are demonstrated, a pendant and a ring, which will help to explain and to provide practice in these basic skills. Jewellery-making techniques are invariably adapted to each specific task as the need arises. Examples of this will be seen in some of the projects later in the book.

SAWING

The most commonly used saw in jewellery-making is probably the piercing saw. This tool can be difficult and often frustrating to use, as the fine blades are very easily broken, but once mastered it will be invaluable.

A cut made with a piercing saw leaves a smooth-sided parallel gap, perfect for soldering.

Internal curves, impossible to cut with shears, are easily achieved with a piercing saw, as are the most complex jigsaw puzzle lines. The finish on the edges left by the piercing saw can be so smooth as to require very little further treatment. There is no bending or distortion of the surface as there is with a sheared cut. Apart from its use in making complex cuts in sheet metal, the piercing saw is also used to saw down an imperfect joint in a broad ring. This cut leaves a smooth-sided parallel gap which, when closed up, makes a perfect joint ready for soldering.

This pattern was cut using a piercing saw.

The key to mastering the piercing saw is choosing the correct blade and keeping a relaxed grip on the handle. The blade should be as fine as possible; a coarse blade with fewer teeth per inch will be more likely to snag, which is the main reason why blades break. The general rule is, the thinner the metal to be sawn, the finer the blade needs to be. There must always be at least two teeth in contact with the sawn edge, to prevent the edge of the metal slipping between two teeth, causing the blade to snag. When fitting a new blade into the frame, fix the far end first with the teeth pointing towards the handle. Then push the frame against the edge of the bench, so that the two ends of the frame move towards each other, and about 3 mm of the unfixed end of the blade moves into the fixing. When the screw is tightened, the frame is released, leaving the blade in tension. The precise sound that is made by flicking the blade with a fingernail cannot be explained in words, but is something you will come to recognise with experience.

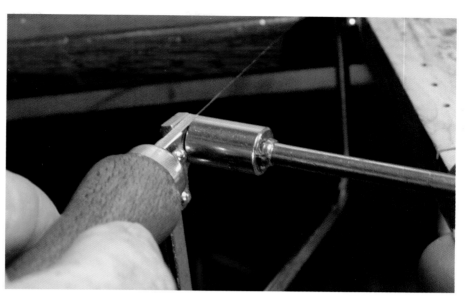

Tighten the screw when the blade is in tension to fix it securely in the frame

Another common cause of blade breakage is gripping the handle too tightly. Every twitch or sudden movement by the user is transmitted to the delicate blade, which is why it can break so easily. The handle should be held so gently that it might seem ready to slip from the grasp. Another important consideration is to use as much of the blade as possible, to ensure that it wears evenly along its length. A common fault is to make short rapid strokes, which limits the wear to a short section of the blade and leads to a narrower cut in the work. When the unworn section of the blade enters this cut it jams, then breaks. Changing the angle of the saw can also often result in blade breakage. The blade should be kept as near vertical as possible, to enable you to recognise any change in its angle. No sudden changes in the direction of the cut should be attempted and any movements should be gradual. The key to success in the use of the piercing saw is to relax, use little force, and let the saw do the work.

A more robust saw which is occasionally used in jewellery-making is the junior hacksaw. Useful for cutting thicker metal, wood and plastic, it will only cut in straight lines and leaves a less tidy edge than that left by the piercing saw. The blade is less likely to break than a piercing-saw blade, making it a cheaper alternative for some of the more straightforward cutting. The teeth on the junior hacksaw blade point away from the handle, so that it cuts on the push stroke.

CUTTING WITH SHEARS AND CUTTERS

Cutting sheet metal with shears, although not providing as tidy an edge as that produced by a piercing saw, can be a quicker alternative. For straight-line cutting, or the cutting of outside curves, the sheared edge is quite acceptable, particularly when subsequent work such as planishing is to be carried out.

Good quality jeweller's shears will be adequate for most purposes if properly looked after, though even a good-quality pair of scissors will cut silver up to 1 mm thick. The blades should be sharpened regularly and the rivet holding them together should be kept tight by regular hammering. In use, shears should never be completely closed until the end of the cut is made. If closed part-way down, the ends of the blades make an unattractive distortion in the cut edge. Greater force is applied by the blade at the end nearest the rivet, so working in short cuts with the blades fairly open is much easier.

When cutting curves it is better to cut to within 1 mm of the line first, using straight cuts. This will allow for the narrow strip that remains to bend away from the shears as the final cut is made.

Making long cuts in thick metal may require larger shears. When a lot of force is needed, it can be easier to hold one handle of the shears in a vice, or else clamp it to the bench. Much more force can be applied by one hand pressing down than by squeezing both handles between fingers and thumb. Even greater force can be generated by extending the length of the top handle using a length of steel tubing.

Shears can be used to cut wire, but this is best done with cutters. These can be side or end cutters. Side cutters are best for thicker wire, as greater force can be applied close to the fulcrum. When a piece of wire is cut, one side of the cut is more pointed than the other. Rather than file this point down, it is easier to cut too much wire, then trim the end with the other side of the cutters. End cutters can be ground flat, removing the little chamfer, which provides for a flatter end.

TIP BECAUSE OF THE CONSIDERABLE FORCE APPLIED, SHEARS CAN SOMETIMES INFLICT PAINFUL INJURIES. FINGERS AND THE BALL OF THE THUMB CAN BE PINCHED BY PARTS OF THE HANDLE. TRY TO BE AWARE OF WHAT IS HAPPENING AT THE HANDLE END WHILE WATCHING THE BLADES.

Cutting sheet metal with shears.

TIP SHEARS CAN BE MORE ECONOMICAL THAN SAWS, AS ANY WASTE THAT IS CREATED WILL BE EASIER TO RECLAIM THAN THE DUST FROM A SAW. THIS IS AN IMPORTANT CONSIDERATION WHEN WORKING WITH PRECIOUS METALS.

When a piece of wire is cut with cutters, the end will be pointed rather than flat.

The end of a piece of wire can be squared off using end cutters.

DRILLING

Before drilling a hole in, say, a pendant, we should decide at what point in the making process it should be drilled. If the hole is made while the metal is flat, and before it is hollowed and planished, the hole and the metal around it may be distorted. This may or may not be desirable, but should be considered, and perhaps tried out on a piece of copper, before silver is used. How far from the edge of the metal the hole is drilled is important. Too far from the edge, and any jump ring in it may have to be too large; too close to the edge will create a weak spot.

Having decided on the position of the hole, make a mark with a permanent pen, roughly the size of the hole and in the place where it is meant to be. The edge of the hole should be no nearer than about 2 mm from the edge of the metal. When you are sure of the size and position of the hole, place the work on a flat steel base and, using a centre punch, make a small indent in the centre of the mark. If necessary, carefully replace the centre punch and repeat the process.

Hold the work securely, either in a vice with a smooth block of wood behind it, or clamped onto a block of wood. Awkward pieces that are difficult to hold in a vice or clamp may be held against a peg or a nail driven into the wood (see p.44 for how to make a drilling clamp to avoid this problem). This will prevent the work spinning round with the drill in the event the drill jams in the hole, which could damage your fingers. Press the drill down firmly into the centre-punch mark but do not force it. Concentrate on keeping the drill upright; ease up as you feel the drill come through the underside of the work.

Any holes made for jump rings should not be too close or too far away from the edge.

When drilling a hole in an awkwardly shaped piece it may be easier to hold it against a nail to prevent it spinning round with the drill.

Drilling a hole with the work held in a vice.

Using a larger drill bit held between finger and thumb, remove the burrs from both sides of the hole with a twisting action (see right). Finally, place the work on a smooth steel block, rest a ball bearing in the hole and strike it firmly with a hammer. This will create a neat little chamfer around the hole (centre right).

Larger holes, 5 mm (¼ in.) or more, are best drilled twice, once with a smaller drill bit to make a pilot hole, then again with the larger one, which will follow the first hole precisely. The drilling of wood and plastic requires slightly different strategies than for metal. Smaller holes in wood are drilled in much the same way as in metal, and centre punching can help to guide the drill into the correct position. For large holes in wood a sharply pointed tip is used to start the drill in the right position.

Plastics such as acrylic cannot be centre-punched, so greater care is needed to start the drill in exactly the right place. Most plastics crack easily, so particular care is required when the drill breaks through the bottom of the hole. Whatever the material being drilled, the task is made much easier when a pedestal drilling machine is used, as this keeps the drill exactly vertical at all times.

Drilling is not always the best way to make a hole. Punching using a punch and die is very effective, particularly for large holes which, when punched, are much neater than drilled holes. There is also a much nicer waste created by the punch and die – little discs that can be recycled to good effect – whereas the drilling process makes swarf, which is difficult to recover and is usually thrown away.

You can elongate a hole using punch and die, nibbling along until you have a slot, something you cannot do with a drill. A piece of steel bolted to a piece of similar-sized plastic makes a very good die, with a broken drill bit, or a piece of a masonry nail, as the punch.

....

TIP   DON'T FORGET THAT MEASURING AND MARKING THE WORK CAN BE DONE REPEATEDLY TO MAKE SURE IT IS RIGHT; THE CUT, RIGHT OR WRONG, CAN ONLY BE MADE ONCE.

....

Removing the burr from the hole with a drill bit.

The pendant on a smooth steel block, with a ball bearing resting in the hole. The ball bearing can be used to give the hole a neat finish.

The hole at the top of this brass pendant was made using a punch and die.

FILING

One of the most common uses for a file is the preparation of an edge after it has been cut with shears. Filing an edge is best done when the work is flat. This makes it easier to hold it securely and to check that the edge is square to the face. Hold the work low down in the vice; you should be looking along the work, not across it. A piece of folded paper or cloth should be wrapped around the work to protect it from the rough jaws. A hand file is used with one hand on the handle and the other hand holding the far end of the file between finger and thumb.

Hold the file at about 45 degrees to the work and parallel to the ground. The file cuts only on the push stroke but should be kept in contact with the metal at all times for greater control. Pause from time to time to check that the file is horizontal. When all the rough corners and hollows have been removed, hold the file at right angles to the work with both thumbs resting on the edge of the file. This is called draw-filing and will produce a smoother finish. Draw-filing is the best way to negotiate curves, and holding the file in this way makes it easier to keep it at right angles to the face.

When filing, hold the file at about 45 degrees to the work.

....

TIP   WHEN FILING, TRY TO USE SLOW DELIBERATE STROKES RATHER THAN RAPID SHORT ONES.

....

A common error when using a file is to hold the work in one hand and the file in the other, making it difficult to tell whether the piece is vertical or horizontal. With the item held in a vice it only remains to keep the file horizontal and the edge will always be square to the face. When an edge is properly filed smooth and square, use emery boards and a burnisher to finish it to a smooth, hard shine.

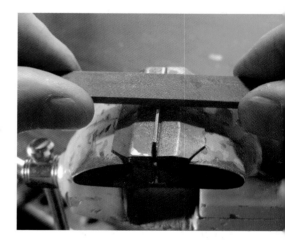

Draw-filing is done by holding the surface of the file at right angles to the edge being filed.

Unless the work is domed, a file is rarely used to remove defects on the face of a project because of the risk of damage to the area surrounding the defect. Faces are best treated with a range of emery boards.

Soft metal can sometimes stick in the teeth of a file. This makes the file less effective and can leave unsightly marks on the work. The problem can be overcome by using a narrow strip of hard brass. Rub it across the file, along the line of the teeth, so that after a few strokes the edge of the brass develops grooves which match the teeth of the file. Continue down along the file, keeping the brass at the same angle, cleaning 10 to 15 rows of teeth with each stroke.

Needle files should only be used in awkward places that are impossible to reach with a conventional file. A needle file, because it is so narrow, can sometimes make unsightly grooves in the work when used on open areas.

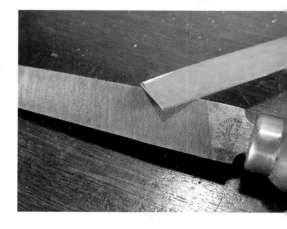

A strip of brass is used to remove soft metal from between the teeth of a file.

BASIC TECHNIQUES PROJECT 1: PLANISHED RING

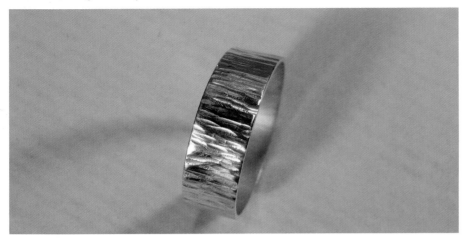

YOU WILL NEED:

◆ 0.8 mm (B&S 20) silver sheet,
7 x 65 mm (¼ x 2½ in.)

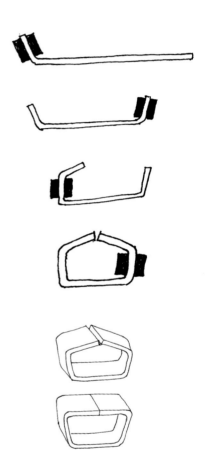

The making of this planished ring demonstrates many of the techniques explained in this section.

1. Having cut the silver strip to size with shears and filed the ends square, bend both ends with pliers. Parallel pliers are best for this purpose. Then, with the pliers held against the first bends, make the second bends as shown in the diagram (right).

2. The final bend is always harder to achieve as the leverage is reduced, so, if necessary hold the work in a vice and use a mallet to make the final bend.

3. Use the mallet again to hammer down the two ends until they meet in a straight line. You may need to employ the piercing saw at this stage to true up the joint (see p.18). With a broad ring of this kind it can be difficult to close the gap completely. It may be necessary to lift up the two sides by pushing the ring onto a ring mandrel, squeezing the ends together in a vice, then tapping them down until they close. Annealing may also be required if repeated attempts cause work-hardening of the metal.

ANNEALING

To snap a piece of wire, it can be bent back and forth repeatedly until it becomes hard and brittle and eventually breaks. This happens because every time metal is worked, whether by bending, twisting or hammering, it becomes harder and eventually further work on it becomes impossible. Silversmiths call this work-hardening. Annealing is the process by which work-hardened metal is restored to a workable condition using heat.

It is important not to overheat silver, either for too long or at too high a temperature. Work in a subdued light, as it can be difficult to judge the colour of the hot metal in ordinary light. This colour should be a dull red, sometimes called cherry red. Thin wire is very easily melted so it should

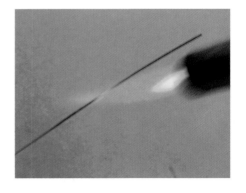

When heating silver wire, look for a dull red colour and then withdraw the heat.

be heated in mid-air, away from any heat-reflecting surfaces. Withdraw the heat as soon as the dull red colour appears.

Thicker sections of metal will take a little longer to reach the required heat.

TIP   WHEN ANNEALING WIRE, MAKE SURE THAT EVERY PART OF THE WIRE IS HEATED, AS ANY HARD AREAS THAT REMAIN WILL LEAD TO UNEVEN BENDING.

Thicker sections of metal will take longer to bring to the required heat and should be maintained at annealing temperature for a little longer. Copper can be quenched in water after heating, but silver, brass and bronze should be left to cool in the air, or placed on a cold block of steel.

SILVER SOLDERING

Soldering is probably the most important, and certainly the most often-used, joining technique when working with silver. Mastery of the process, and in particular of the soldering torch, is in many ways the key to success in jewellery-making. There is more danger involved in soldering than at any other stage in the making process. The high temperatures involved make melting, not just of the solder but of the work as a whole, a genuine risk.

Silver solder is an alloy containing silver and other metals, mainly copper and zinc; the presence of zinc lowers the melting point of the alloy. There are five grades of silver solder: extra easy, easy, medium, hard and enamelling. Solders of different melting points are needed when more than one soldering stage is carried out on the same piece. A solder with a high melting point is used for the first join, so that when subsequent joins are made the first one will not re-melt. Extra-easy solder, which has the lowest melting point, is used mainly on repairs, making it unlikely that existing joins will be melted. Enamelling-grade solder is used for work that will be enamelled later, a process involving extreme heat. For most purposes no more than two grades, easy and hard, will be needed.

Health and safety notes

Always clear any inflammable material from the area where soldering is carried out.

Never leave a soldering torch alight when it is not being used.

A piece of metal need not be red to cause a nasty burn. Always assume the work is hot and use tongs or tweezers to move it.

Never put hot metal into the acid pickle. The vapour created can cause damage to eyes, skin and clothes.

Preparation is the key to good soldering practice. For successful soldering the joint must be a good fit, it must be clean, flux must be applied and the heat properly directed. Molten solder has the consistency of water, and like water it will flow into tiny gaps by capillary action, but it will not fill up wider gaps.

Pallions should be placed across the joint, touching both sides.

Point the flame onto the joint only when the solder begins to melt.

Unless both sides of the join touch completely, the soldered joint will be unsatisfactory. Molten solder will not flow on to greasy or oxide-coated metal, as when it melts, the solder will ball up like water droplets on a highly polished surface.

Before soldering, the metal must be thoroughly cleaned with emery paper or a scraper, and not handled with fingers which may be greasy. Whenever metal is heated, oxides form on the surface which would inhibit the flow of solder. A flux is used which creates a barrier between the metal and the flame, preventing the formation of oxides and allowing the solder to flow.

The hottest part of the flame is towards the end, just beyond the blue cone (see arrow).

To prepare flux, grind the borax cone in the borax dish with water until the mixture is about the consistency of milk. Too much water and the coating will be too thin and may burn away before the solder flows; if the mixture is too creamy, the coating will be so thick as to obscure the melting solder, which might be melting in the wrong place.

Solder is used in the form of small flakes called pallions; these are coated with flux and placed across the joint, touching both sides. The size of a pallion depends on the size of the work but is usually 1–1.5 mm square. Set the work on the soldering block so that it can be brought to the required heat as quickly as possible. The flame should be allowed to flow under and around the work and to reflect off the surrounding surfaces.

Speed is important, as the flux will gradually lose its effectiveness under the intense heat. The hottest part of the flame is towards the tip, just beyond the blue cone. The cone itself is not hot, being composed of unburnt gas. The flame should be directed away from the join at first until the whole piece is red-hot. Point the flame onto the join just as the solder begins to melt; this will preserve the flux for as long as possible. Watch carefully for the solder to flow into a flat pool and then quickly withdraw the flame.

After the soldering process is finished, the spent flux which remains forms a hard, glass-like coating which can only be removed using chemicals. As soon as the work is no longer red, quench it in water. This often helps to dislodge spent flux. When it is cold, place the work in the acid pickle using copper tongs or tweezers, or fasten it to a length of copper wire and lower it in. Never put iron or steel into the acid pickle, as this will cause a copper coating to form on the surface of silver.

Placing the work in acid pickle using a length of copper wire.

PLANISHING

Planishing is the forming of metal using hammers to harden and polish the surface. The marks left by the hammer add character to the work, making a planished finish far superior to a smooth, mirror-like surface.

When all the spent flux has been dissolved by the acid pickle, the ring can be made round on the ring mandrel. Use a mallet for this process, as it will not stretch the ring or mark the surface of the silver. Direct the mallet to wherever there is a gap between the ring and the mandrel.

With the ring more or less round the planishing process can begin. Here a bark-like texture is being created by means of a cross-peen hammer. The ring will become stretched by this process, so it must be checked for size as the work progresses.

When the outside surface has a regular and even texture, the edges of the ring can be made smooth in preparation for polishing. Holding the ring between finger and thumb, rub each edge on an emery board, or on a sheet of emery paper held on a flat surface. When all the distortions caused by the planishing have been smoothed out, repeat the process on an extra-fine emery board to make the surface ready for the polishing stage.

Using a hide mallet to make the ring round on the ring mandrel.

Planishing with a cross-peen hammer.

The planished ring ready for polishing.

BASIC TECHNIQUES PROJECT 2: BRONZE PENDANT

This project provides some practice in using the piercing saw, and in planishing. Bronze is a beautiful metal with many attractions for the jewellery maker; as it is inexpensive it is ideal for practice projects. The shape of this pendant was arrived at by drawing round a dessert spoon.

When planishing a flat sheet, you should first hollow the work slightly, then planish it on the outside or domed side. If a flat sheet is planished, the slight stretching in the middle causes hollowing from the front, which can be difficult to control. Silversmiths use a bossing mallet and a sandbag for the hollowing process. These tools can be expensive, and once bought are often little used. So hollowing can also be done with a punch made from a piece of broom handle, rounded at the end with the metal supported on a yielding surface, such as a telephone directory or a pile of newspapers.

Both planishing hammer and stake are domed slightly and highly polished. The dome on the hammer will, of course, determine the kind of pattern produced. Position the work over a leg of the bench for greater support.

The rounded end of a broom handle can be used to hollow a flat surface prior to planishing.

Begin in the centre of the work with the hammer coming down squarely over the centre of the stake. The metal should be trapped between hammer and stake with no space between. The dull sound made will be easily recognised, when compared to the hollow sound heard when the metal is not in contact with the stake. The work is moved around on the stake – the hammer always comes down over the same spot on the stake.

TIP   TRY TO COVER THE ENTIRE SURFACE, LEAVING NO UNHAMMERED SECTIONS; THESE WILL SHOW UP CLEARLY AS DULL AREAS ON THE SURFACE OF THE FINISHED PIECE.

If planishing continues right up to the edge of the work it may become distorted, so the edges must be treated separately. The best way to handle them is to create a bevel. Hold the work with its edge just short of one side of the centre of the stake and with the hammer slightly overlapping it (see right). Use a permanent pen to draw a line on the steel as a guide to help to keep the work in position. Work around the edge very slowly; try to keep the hammer in the same position relative to the edge all the way round.

FORGING

A distinction can be made between planishing and forging, in that planishing is surface embellishment and decoration, while forging involves a more radical change in the shape of the metal. Before beginning forging it is well to remember two important facts. The first is that four or five carefully aimed hammer blows will be just as effective as one heavy blow, which might miss. The second thing to bear in mind is that there is no such thing as unhammering. Once you have hammered your silver so that it is paper thin, there is no going back.

TIP   THE HAMMER ALWAYS COMES DOWN VERTICALLY. NEVER TRY TO HAMMER SIDEWAYS, NOT EVEN AT AN ANGLE.

BENDING

Bending usually involves wire, and is the basis of many jewellery projects. Hands, pliers or a vice can be used, as well as bending jigs, either general-purpose ones or those made for a specific task such as ear wires. The method chosen will depend on the type of bend needed and the thickness and toughness of the metal. A metal surface is easily damaged when a lot of force is applied, so, as with many other tasks, wooden tools are often preferred to metal ones.

Where there is no alternative to metal pliers or a vice, then sharp corners on the jaws should be rounded off, and even polished, to make them more metal-friendly. Copper vice guards are always useful, and even heavy-duty pliers can be guarded with copper.

POLISHING

The finishing and polishing of jewellery projects is time-consuming. However long it takes to construct a project, the polishing stage will almost always take longer. Work can easily be ruined by taking shortcuts at this stage. Most polishing takes the form of abrading using successively finer abrasives. Deeper scratches and imperfections are removed by making finer scratches until a smooth surface is achieved.

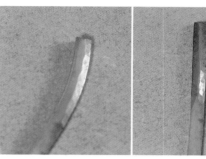

A simple test on a piece of scrap metal provides a useful illustration of the effect forging can have. Take a strip of copper or brass about 4 mm wide and 1 mm thick (18 B&S) and hammer it down one side only. Note how the metal bends away from the side being hammered (LEFT). No metal is removed by the hammer, so what gets thinner in one dimension must get longer in another, and thus it bends. If the other side is hammered the strip will return to straight again, but be slightly longer (RIGHT).

TIP   WHEN THE WORK IS HELD IN A VICE, BOTH HANDS ARE LEFT FREE TO BEND THE METAL, ALLOWING GREATER FORCE TO BE APPLIED WITH MORE CONTROL.

During construction, some consideration may need to be given to the polishing stage. For example, when a hammered finish is the aim, the work should be given a preliminary polish before planishing so that very little polishing will be needed later. In this way the marks of the hammer will be preserved.

Prevention is better than cure. Try to avoid needless restoration by taking good care of work in progress. Have a soft cloth available on which to place work, and wherever possible cover the areas not being worked on with masking tape. Take care that all polishing tools are clean: a minute speck of grit on a polishing pad or mop will create damage which could take hours to put right. Clean the work thoroughly with soap and water between each stage of the finishing process.

Emery boards are used first in the finishing process. Try to use them at different angles and from different directions, as repeated strokes of an emery board in the same spot can create unwanted grooves which are difficult to remove. Wherever possible change the direction of the stroke with each change of grade, working at right angles to the previous stage. This will make it easier to tell whether coarser scratches are being removed and replaced by finer ones. Water of Ayr stone or slate is used with water for awkward places which cannot be reached with emery boards.

When the surface is smooth enough, you can begin to use the polishing machine. Trial and error is the only way to decide when the work is smooth enough. Between each stage, make a careful examination with an eyeglass under a good light. If the grooves are still visible from the previous stage you will need to revert to a fine emery board, as trying to remove scratches with polish, or too fine an abrasive, can be a waste of time.

....

TIP   OPERATING THE POLISHING MACHINE IS EXTREMELY DIRTY WORK AND AN EXTRA OVERALL IS A GOOD IDEA, ESPECIALLY WHEN USING THE MACHINE OVER A LONG PERIOD.

....

The polishing machine can often be a stumbling block, where mistakes can happen and work can be spoiled. Complete concentration is required at all times. **Long hair must be tied back, apron strings tied behind, and bracelets or loose cuffs, which may become entangled in the wheel, should be removed. These are all important safety considerations.** Removing your watch and rolling up long sleeves will make washing your hands easier.

It is easy for the fast-moving wheel to drag the work from the hands so keep a firm grip. Try to move the work around to allow the wheel to move across it in different directions. Use the bottom front quarter of the wheel,

Hammer marks enliven the surface of these pieces.

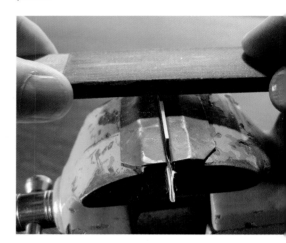

Emery boards are used first in the finishing process.

Polishing the pendant using a polishing machine.

as this will allow the piece to be more easily seen and, should it come out of your hand, it will be thrown away from you. Wherever possible apply the wheel to the trailing edge of the metal, working from the centre towards the edge.

Thin metal or wire projects, which might bend when pressed against the polishing wheel, must be supported against a piece of wood.

Try not to polish the corners and edges excessively; it is easy to round off prominent points while trying to polish around them. Edges and corners are best treated by burnishing or planishing. Hammering the edge of a handheld piece of work, known as caulking, will both polish and harden the metal. This is a good thing, as edges and corners are subject to more wear than other parts of the piece.

A common mistake when using of the polishing machine is to hold the work too much at arm's length. Not being afraid of the machine, and standing close to it, with the expectation of polishing fingers, is the best way to keep control of the work.

It is most important to apply the polish a little at a time, but often. The polishing block is composed of a fine abrasive in a waxlike binder. The abrasive element is the first to wear off the wheel, leaving the wax behind. This residue can build up on the work unless the abrasive is constantly replenished, a little at a time. The wheel will only absorb so much polish; once it is fully covered any excess polish you apply will be wasted.

Lengths of wire or loose chain must never be polished on a polishing machine. A chain entangled in a polishing mop can do severe damage. The best way to polish a chain is with powdered rouge on a cloth. Fasten the end of the chain to the bench with a nail, so that the chain can be pulled straight with one hand.

Powdered rouge can also be used on polishing pads, or strips of leather, to get into awkward corners that are difficult to reach with the machine. An advantage of powdered rouge is that it is more easily cleaned off the work than the waxed block. A bundle of string, covered with polish and tied to the bench, can be used to polish inside holes and tight corners. Thread the work on to one or more strands of string, hold the string taut, and rub the work back and forth along it.

The final stage in the polishing process is a good wash using soft soap, or washing-up liquid, with a soft brush, such as an old toothbrush. Stubborn bits of polish lodged in corners can be poked out using a cocktail stick.

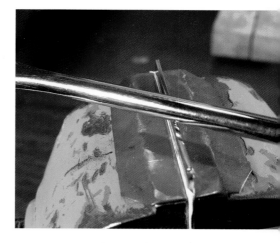

The edge of a piece of work is often best treated by burnishing.

TIP KEEP THE VARIOUS GRADES OF ABRASIVE AND POLISHES AND POLISHING TOOLS SEPARATE FROM ONE ANOTHER, SO THAT FINER POLISHES ARE NOT CONTAMINATED BY COARSER ONES.

TIP POWDERED ROUGE IS INCREDIBLY DIRTY. MIXING IT WITH WATER INTO A THIN PASTE HELPS TO KEEP IT FROM SPREADING ALL OVER THE WORKSHOP.

3 The making of simple specialised tools

HOLDING DEVICES

IN JEWELLERY-MAKING, MORE SO THAN IN MANY other crafts, holding devices are especially important. Jewellery is very often small and difficult to grip securely. Sometimes considerable force must be applied to the work, demanding that you hold it firmly. A device that holds the piece securely, and without requiring any effort, can be invaluable. The next few pages show several very different holding tools, and how to use them to make some simple projects.

The first item is a little hand vice, which is both dedicated to a specific task, such as squaring off the ends of wire, and versatile, in that it will hold securely any thickness of sheet or wire likely to be used in the making of jewellery. Made of wood, it will cause less wear on files and saws than a metal vice, and can be adapted as the need arises by drilling and filing. Wooden tools are more easily made in a home workshop, and are also warmer and more comfortable to use.

1. Mark out the wood as shown in the diagram (opposite) and drill two holes 6.5 and 10 mm (¼ and ³/₈ in.) in diameter. Place a smooth piece of scrap wood under the work to prevent the underside of the holes splitting.

YOU WILL NEED:

♦ Hardwood block 150 x 20 x 20 mm (6 x ¾ x ¾ in.). You may prefer to start with a longer piece, to allow for mistakes, and then trim it to length.

♦ 30 mm (1⅛ in.) cup square M6 bolt with nut and washer

Sawing the slot in the hand vice using two blades in the hacksaw.

2. Make the saw cut down the centre; a band saw will make this task easy, but two blades side by side in a hacksaw frame will also work if a band saw is not available. Smooth the inside of the jaws with a piece of folded glass paper.

3. Insert the cup square bolt into the 6.5 mm (¼ in.) hole and tighten the nut to force the square section into it. If necessary, use a hammer to force it completely home. Cut off the outside corners at the ends of the jaws to make the shape shown in the diagram (front view), and smooth with glass paper.

BENDING JIG WITH NAILS

The making of the little hand vice will make it easy to carry out the first stage of the ring-making project, which is to file the ends of the wire flat and square. The next stage will be to bend the wire into shape. Pliers can be used for this process, but a simple bending jig will enable this task, and many more like it, to be carried out more easily. The bends will be more rounded, and there will be less risk of damage to the surface of the metal.

1. Begin by marking out the wood as shown in the diagram on the following page (top). Having set out all the centre points of the holes, score lines across the wood using a knife, then colour alternate stripes in ink. Drill all of the 4 mm holes all the way through.

2. The remaining sets of four holes are blind holes ranging in depth from 7 to 10 mm (¼ to ³⁄₈ in.). The easiest way to drill these holes is with a pillar drill and a pack of playing cards. Set the depth of the drill to the top surface of the wood. Take a stack of cards 7 mm (¼ in.) high, and insert it under the work to raise it up. Drill the first hole.

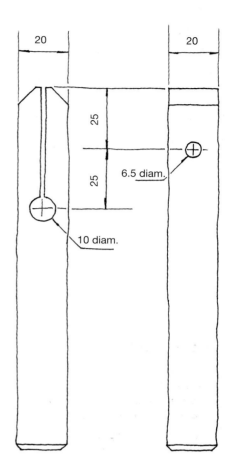

Diagram and measurements for a hand vice (front view, left; side view, right). All dimensions are in mm.

YOU WILL NEED:

- Hardwood block, 250 x 60 x 20 mm (10 x 2³⁄₈ x ¾ in.)
- Six 75 mm (3 in.) round nails
- Two acrylic strips, 175 x 25 x 6 mm (7 x 1 x ¼ in.)
- One piece of plywood, approx. 100 x 20 x 20 mm (4 x ¾ x ¾ in.)
- Four pieces of card, approx. 100 x 60 x 1 mm (to be used as guides), or a pack of playing cards

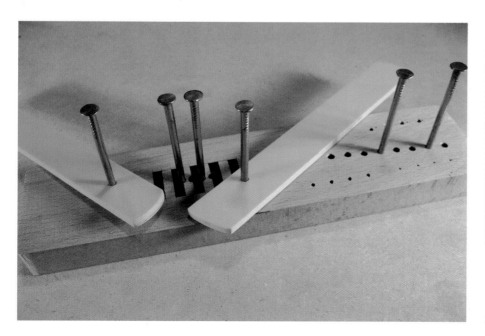

A simple bending jig.

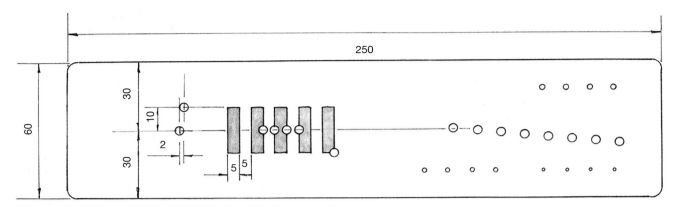

ABOVE **Measurements for the jig with nails.** RIGHT **Levers, not shown full length. All dimensions are in mm.**

Add more cards to the stack to increase the height of the work to 8 mm, and drill the next hole, and so on for the remaining holes.

If a pedestal drill is not available, use a block of wood 100 mm x 60 mm x 20 mm, (4 in x 2½ in x ¾ in) as a depth guide. Drill a line of four 1.5 mm holes in the guide. Position the drill bit in the drill with 30 mm (1¼ in) protruding from the chuck (see picture below right).

With the guide in position on the work, drill through the first hole until the chuck rests on the depth guide. This will make a hole 10 mm (³/₈ in) deep. Place a piece of card 1 mm under the guide and drill the second hole in the same way to make a hole 9 mm deep.

Drill the remaining two holes with an extra layer of card under each to make holes of 8 mm and 7 mm. Repeat this process with drills of 2 mm and 2.5 mm, for the remaining sets of blind holes.

3. Drill the holes in the acrylic strips to make the levers for the jig, then file them to shape and make the ends smooth.

4. Round off the ends of the nails and polish them so that they slide freely in and out of the holes.

FORGED SILVER RING: PART 1

The ring is the basis of most jewellery. The finger ring, the links of a chain, even the setting for a stone, all involve the joining, by soldering, of each end of a length of metal. Making this forged ring should bring an appreciation of the effectiveness of the soldering process, as the join will be fully tested by the subsequent forging. The use of fairly thick wire lessens the chances of the work melting.

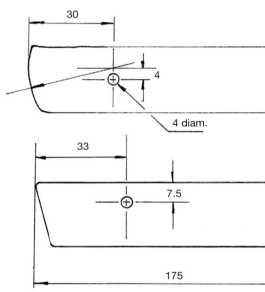

YOU WILL NEED:

◆ 2 mm (B&S 12) silver wire, 55 mm (2⅛ in.) long

◆ Wooden hand vice (see pp.32–3)

◆ Bending jig (see p.33 and above)

The first task of any soldering job is to ensure that the two sides of the join fit together perfectly with no gaps in between. This can be achieved by using the two simple tools we have made.

1. Begin by squaring off both ends of the wire. Hold it in the wooden hand vice with just the irregularly shaped section protruding beyond the surface of the wood. File the wire until the end is flush with the wood. Expect to file the side of the vice. Remove the burr from each end with a small piece of folded emery paper.

2. Bend each end of the wire using the second deepest blind hole of the 2.5 mm row as a guide.

3. Place the wire in the bending jig, using the stripes to make sure it is in the centre, and then lock it in place with a nail.

4. Use the lever to bend one side in two stages, first with the upper hole as the fulcrum, then with the lower hole. Turn the ring over and do the same to the other end.

5. Using a hide mallet, carefully tap down the two ends until they come together in a straight line.

7. Begin the soldering process by bending a length of iron wire into a U-shape; a paper clip is ideal for this purpose. Paint the joint with flux and then place it on the charcoal block or firebrick with the paper clip under it.

The forged silver ring.

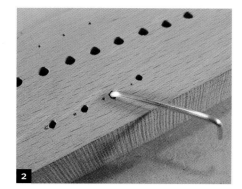

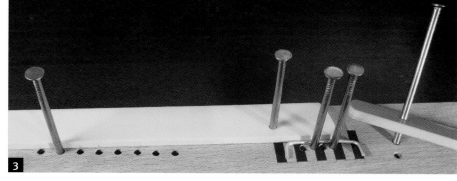

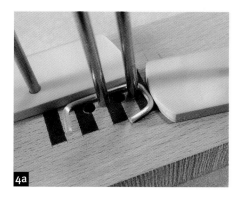

The join should be on the far side, away from the flame. Place a pallion of easy solder across the join.

8. Heat the back of the work to begin with, and allow the heat to conduct round to the join. Only when the whole work is red and the pallion begins to melt should the flame be directed onto the join.

9. The work should now be cooled, and then placed in the acid pickle to dissolve the spent flux.

Heat the back of the wire until the solder has melted. Keep the flame square to the work, watching the colour change, to ensure that both sides are heated evenly.

Points to note

- Raising the work on the paperclip allows the flame to reach under the work, reflecting off the surface of the fire brick and heating the work more quickly. Speed is important in soldering as the flux can sometimes burn away before the solder has properly melted.
- Heating away from the join to begin with ensures that the work as a whole gets hot, with little degrading of the flux.
- If the joint were heated first, the pallion, being smaller, would melt into a ball and perhaps roll out of position. This is known as 'balling-up'.

CHAIN STAY RING MANDREL

The next stage in the making of a ring requires a ring mandrel. This is quite an expensive item of equipment, but one which can be made at home quite cheaply. This one is made from the chain stay of a bicycle frame, the section which runs alongside the chain.

YOU WILL NEED:
- Bicycle chain stay
- Pewter
- Bucket of dry sand
- Ladle
- Small camping stove
- Safety goggles

Most council tips will have at least one old bike (but ask for permission first before taking anything away). Alternatively, a bike shop may have an old frame, perhaps damaged, which is surplus to requirements.

1. Begin by sawing both ends of the chain stay square with a hack saw. Saw off any cable guides and file the surface smooth. Burn off the paint, and then, while it is still warm, push the narrow end into the bucket of dry sand.

2. Melt a small amount of pewter in the ladle and, wearing goggles, pour it into the chain stay. Pour dry sand into the tube to a depth of about 2 or 3 cm (¾ to 1¼ in.) from the top and ram it down firmly. Reheat the metal to make sure there is no moisture present, then fill the remaining space with molten metal.

3. Shake out any sand from the narrow end of the tube and top up the space with molten metal, bearing in mind the safety advice given below.

Safety advice

When cold metal is heated, condensation appears on the surface. If this moisture is present when molten metal is poured, the metal will spit, sometimes violently, and in some cases an explosion will occur. Therefore, only melt as much as you need, wear goggles, and warm the work thoroughly before pouring.

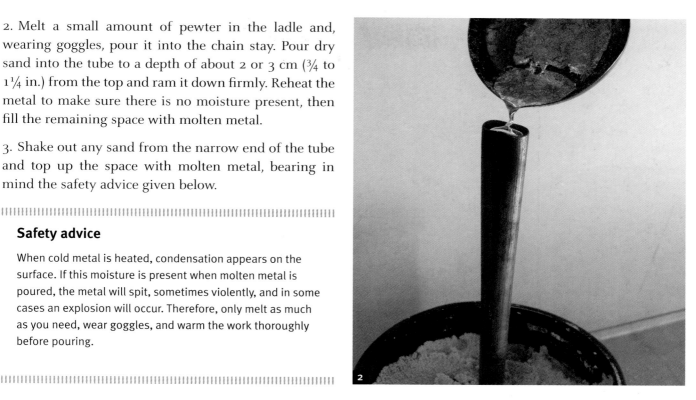

FORGED SILVER RING: PART 2

To complete the forged ring (started on p.34) we must first make it round.

1. Using a mallet, lightly tap the edges to create a shape that will fit over the end of the mandrel. Then, resting the mandrel on the edge of the bench, hammer any part where you see a gap under the ring, until it is round. To make sure the ring is flat, hammer it firmly with a mallet against a block of hardwood.

2. Begin the forging process by hammering the top of the ring to create a flat section on the top of the ring. Hold the mandrel firmly, close to the ring, pressing it down against a flat steel stake. This will create a smaller flat exactly opposite the first one.

3. Turn the work over and hammer the smaller flat until it matches the first one. Try to feel the original flat in position against the stake, to ensure that the two flats are exactly opposite one another. Repeat this process to create four equal flats at ninety degrees to each other.

4. Make a mark with a permanent pen exactly in the centre of each of the four unhammered sections; these dots will be the only parts of the work which must not be touched by the hammer.

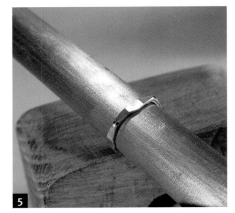

5. Next, hammer a small flat area at each end of the four original flats. As the flat stake is no longer in use, hold the work much closer to your body for better control of the hammer and greater accuracy. Position the work so that you can see the light as it reflects off the section being hammered.

6. Lightly planish each of the four faces, starting with the two ridges, until the flat sections blend gradually into the four corners.

7. Polish the inside of the ring, at first with fine emery paper held in a split dowel, then with a strip of leather in a dowel, coated with rouge. Finally, thread the ring onto a length of rope coated with rouge and rub it vigorously up and down.

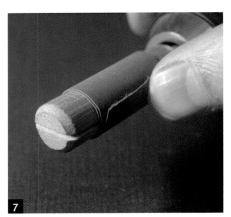

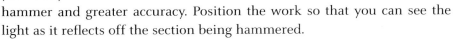

Points to note

- A mallet will only bend wire, not stretch it or change its section.
- To avoid stretching the ring too much, check your work regularly. Forging is a process in which it is easy to get carried away.
- Several carefully aimed blows with a hammer are better than one heavy, inaccurate blow.

RING-SIZING STICK

Ring-sizing is an imperfect science: rings are round, while fingers are not. Fingers can swell and shrink, being generally larger at the end of the day. Knuckles must also be considered; a broad flat ring will not pass over a knuckle as easily as a narrow ring.

There are many different ways of measuring ring sizes. It may be that the size is known, as when an existing ring is to be matched. Alternatively, the finger of the wearer may have to be measured. The UK system, where each size of ring is designated a letter from A to Z, is useful, as are all other universally accepted systems. Most people know, for example, what is meant by a size S. (See the ring-sizing table on p.140 for a list of sizes.)

YOU WILL NEED:

- ◆ 300 x 25 mm (12 x 1 in.) strip of acrylic or similar hard plastic
- ◆ Set of ring sizers
- ◆ Small sheet of plywood
- ◆ Strip of wood

To make the graduations on the tapered acrylic strip square to its centre, it is necessary to make this simple jig. The tapered acrylic strip is positioned so that a line drawn down its centre is parallel to the bottom edge of the board. A thin strip of wood is then nailed to the board at a slight angle to keep the acrylic strip in position. A try-square can then be used to mark the graduations for each ring size at right angles to the centre line of the acrylic strip (see picture top right p.40).

To determine the length of metal required to make a ring of a given size, thread the ring or ring-sizer onto a ring mandrel and mark its position with a permanent pen. Take a length of thin wire, wrap it around the point on the mandrel and twist the ends to form a ring. Cut the wire and open it out into a straight line, and you will have the length of metal needed.

To measure a finger, use the same method, or use a length of adhesive tape. Wrap the wire or tape around the knuckle and mark the point at which it overlaps. When you unwind it, or peal it off, you have the length, provided you avoid stretching the wire or tape.

A ring stick can be made from a ring mandrel by simply marking each point on the mandrel using a set of sizing rings, then filing a groove at each point. If filing a groove on your ring mandrel is unacceptable, then make a flat ring-sizing stick, which measures ring diameter. On one side mark the letter sizes, and on the other the length for each ring blank.

The only requirement when cutting out this stick is that each edge must be flat and smooth with no bumps or hollows. The angle or taper does not matter, but the more gradual the taper is, the further apart the graduations will be.

1. Cut off the edge of the acrylic to form a taper, being 12 mm (½ in.) wide at the narrow end. Finish both edges to make them perfectly straight and polished.

2. Using the ring sizers, mark the position of each size on the acrylic with a permanent pen.

3. Lay the work out on the plywood with the centre line of the tapered work piece parallel with the wooden strip (see right). With the try-square resting on the bottom edge of the board, the lines made will be at right angles to the centre line of the work piece. With a needle file, make a small groove on each side of each mark. Scratch each letter in the appropriate place, or use an engraving burr. You may find it's unnecessary to engrave every letter, only every second or third one.

4. To make the graduations on the other side, use the chart on p.140 to determine the position of each point, then square off and file each mark as before. Rub over all the marks with a permanent pen, and then clean off the face to show the marks more clearly.

It is worth remarking that this tool, while flat, is no less accurate than a round one, as the ring will always take the line of least resistance down the middle, its true diameter.

It should always be remembered that many rings will be planished or worked in a way that will stretch the metal, so allowance must be made for this. In many cases the only way to be sure a finished ring is the right size will be to make a model in base metal.

COMPRESSION RING WITH BEAD

Most people, when asked to break a piece of wire, would simply bend it back and forth repeatedly until it breaks. Fewer people would be able to explain why the wire breaks. When metal is bent, twisted or hammered, it becomes increasingly hard and brittle. Silversmiths call this work-hardening, and when it happens it is usually necessary to soften the metal by annealing.

A certain amount of hardness in a metal is desirable, giving it more

YOU WILL NEED:

- ◆ 2 mm (B&S 12) silver wire, approx. 55 mm (2¹/₈ in.) long
- ◆ Wooden hand vice (see pp.32–3)
- ◆ Bending jig (see pp.33–4)
- ◆ Ring mandrel (see pp.36–7)
- ◆ Bead

resistance to dents and scratches, but for this ring it is essential. In this project the springiness of the metal ensures that the bead is held in place by compression. There are too many variables in this design of ring to be certain of its finished size. However, if a specific size is needed, the best procedure is to make a model in copper, noting down the exact length of the original wire.

1. Begin by bending the ends of the wire in the 8 mm blind hole of the bending jig (see p.35), trying to make both ends the same angle.

2. Hold the work in the hand vice and file the ends to a three-sided point.

3. Bend the wire until both ends meet – you may need to use a mallet for this. Thread the ring onto a ring mandrel and lightly planish it until it fits the round mandrel. This will probably make the ring too open, so close it up with your fingers or a mallet, and planish it again.

4. Continue this process until the ring is sufficiently springy to allow it to be pulled apart while still being able to spring back to its original position. The gap should be a little less than the size of the bead. Polish the ring thoroughly, making sure that you blunt the sharp points.

TIP   MORE THAN ONE BEAD CAN BE USED, BUT IN THIS CASE A SHORT LENGTH OF WIRE IS NEEDED TO HOLD THE BEADS TOGETHER. THIS MUST BE A TIGHT FIT THROUGH THE HOLES IN THE BEADS, AND SHORT ENOUGH TO LEAVE ROOM FOR THE POINTS OF THE RING TO HOLD THE BEADS SECURELY.

The flat, plastic ring-sizing tool makes the changing of beads much easier. Clamp the tapered strip to the bench and slide the open ring along it until the bead can be positioned in the gap. When the ring is slid down the taper, the bead will be held securely.

The same principle that holds the bead in place can be used to hold other shaped stones. In the picture below left, a 4 mm square-faceted cabochon is held in an oval wire ring. The easiest way to make this version is to solder the ring closed, planish the surface all over to harden it, then cut down the join with a piercing saw. The ring can now be opened sideways to allow the flat ends to be drilled with 1 mm holes in which the corners of the stone will sit.

The ring's flat ends are drilled with 1 mm holes, in which the corners of the stone will sit.

BENCH PEG MODIFICATIONS AND OTHER HOLDING TOOLS

Almost any process is made more difficult if the work is not firmly held. It is also more dangerous; a high proportion of accidents happen when a piece comes loose from whatever is holding it, sometimes the operator's hand. With the work securely held, two hands can be used to control the tool more effectively. A range of holding devices is every bit as important as cutting, drilling, hammering or polishing tools.

Two modifications to the bench peg provide more holding options. The first example turns the bench peg into a vice. With this device it is easy to true up edges. The second modification is the addition of a lever, which allows sheet material to be held securely – particularly useful when drilling.

BENCH PEG MODIFICATION 1

This device is especially useful when truing up the ends of broad ring blanks.

> **YOU WILL NEED:**
>
> ◆ Bench peg
> ◆ 60 mm (2³/₈ in.) M6 bolt with nut and washer

1. Begin by drilling a 6.5 mm (¼ in.) hole from one side of the bench peg to the other, and counter-bore one end to 10 mm (³/₈ in.).

2. With the M6 nut held against the 10 mm (³/₈ in.) hole, thread the M6 bolt through from the opposite side to engage with it. Tighten the bolt to pull the nut into the 10 mm (³/₈ in.) hole, making a deep impression around the edge.

3. Cut out the remains of the wood in the six corners with a chisel or a craft knife, and force the nut into place by fully tightening the bolt. Use epoxy adhesive if necessary to fix it permanently.

The bolt must be removable to allow the piercing saw into the slot.

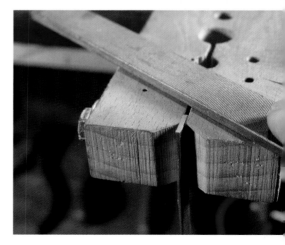

ABOVE RIGHT **The nut is forced into the hole by tightening the bolt.**

RIGHT **Tightening the bolt secures the work within the slot.**

BENCH PEG MODIFICATION 2

Holding sheet material for drilling is one of the main uses for this bench peg modification. Making the two bolts long enough leaves room for a piece of waste material under the work to protect the bench peg from the drill. The ease with which this clamp can be tightened and released also makes it useful in certain piercing operations.

YOU WILL NEED:

♦ Hardwood or plywood strip,
  90 x 20 x 15 mm (3½ x ¾ x ⅝ in.)
  (for the lever)

♦ Two 50 mm (2 in.) M6 bolts with nuts
  and washers

♦ Bench peg

♦ 50 mm (2 in.) length of plywood, cut
  to the same width as the bench peg
  (for the underside of the bench peg)

TIP TO MAKE IT EASIER TO TIGHTEN AND LOOSEN THE CLAMP, A PIECE OF PLYWOOD CAN BE FIXED TO THE BOLT AT THE END OF THE LEVER (SEE PICTURE LEFT). THE NUT ON THE UNDERSIDE HAS BEEN FORCED INTO THE PLYWOOD TO MAKE A DEEP IMPRINT.

1. This modification involves the making of a wooden lever. Drill three 6.5 mm (¼ in.) holes into the strip, one 12 mm (½ in.) from one end, and the others 45 and 30 mm (1¾ and 1⅛ in.) from the opposite end.

2. Counter-bore the first hole to 10 mm (⅜ in.) and force an M6 nut into place, in the same way as for bench peg modification 1.

3. Saw the other end, sloping down to about 5 mm thick at the end.

4. Drill a 6.5 mm (¼ in.) hole in the bench peg about 20 mm (¾ in.) beyond the large hole.

5. Taking the plywood cut for the underside of the bench peg, drill a 10 mm (⅜ in.) hole near the edge and saw down to it to make a slot into which an M6 nut will fit tightly. Glue the plywood to the underside of the bench peg with the bolt in place on the nut.

6. The hardwood lever can now be threaded onto the bolt; another bolt threaded into the captive nut at the end of the lever will generate enough force to secure the work. Greater force will, of course, be applied to the work when using the hole close to the end of the lever.

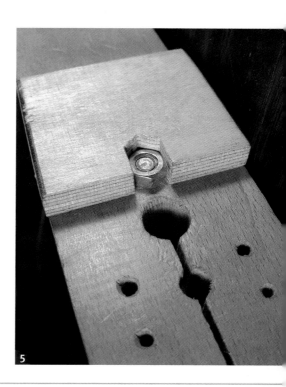

5

A DRILLING CLAMP

It is probably true to say that more minor accidents happen during drilling operations than during any other processes. The drill can often become jammed in the hole, usually just as it bursts through the underside of the metal. When this happens the work can spin round with the drill at great speed, causing damage to the work and to the fingers of the operator.

This simple holding tool is so easy and cheap to make that it can be replaced again and again when both sides of the base become full of holes.

1. Drill a hole in the centre of the board in which the dowel is a good fit; you should be able to push it in and out with firm thumb pressure.

....

TIP   ONE WAY OF MAKING A DOWEL FIT A HOLE IS TO DRILL A SIMILAR HOLE IN A PIECE OF HARDWOOD, AND TO HAMMER THE DOWEL BACK AND FORTH THROUGH THE HOLE UNTIL ITS SURFACE IS SMOOTH AND PERFECTLY ROUND.

....

2. Make a saw cut in the side of the dowel to about halfway through and at a height equal to the thickness of the plywood base; it is important that the dowel does not protrude beyond the bottom of the base so that it cannot be pushed up accidentally during use.

To use the device, place a thin piece of metal in the saw cut and push the dowel down into the hole to hold the metal in place.

A drill turns clockwise, so the work should always be positioned so that, if it came loose, it would move into the saw cut rather than away from the dowel. The saw cut will also prevent the work from being drawn up the drill as sometimes happens. The base is large enough to be safely held in the hand, or it can be clamped to the bench.

YOU WILL NEED:

♦ Plywood, 12 x 100 x 100 mm (½ x 4 x 4 in.)

♦ Dowel of 12 mm (½ in.) diameter, about 30 mm (1⅛ in.) long

The drilling clamp in use.

The dowel removed from the hole in the board to reveal the saw cut.

WINE-BOTTLE MANDREL

When two metals are rubbed against each other, the harder of the two will make a mark on the other. When the harder metal is highly polished, the mark made will also have a high polish. This process, known as burnishing, is used either in combination with, or instead of, the abrading processes, where the metal is worn away by a succession of abrasives, each one finer than the last.

TIP BURNISHING HAS THE ADVANTAGE OVER ABRADING IN THAT NO METAL IS REMOVED; IT IS THE ONLY WAY IN WHICH GOLD LEAF MAY BE POLISHED.

CHOKER

To the resourceful jewellery maker, potential tools and useful devices are everywhere, whether in the kitchen, the garage or the DIY store. To make a silver choker we need look no further than a sparkling wine bottle and a piece of cutlery.

Any wine bottle with a gradual taper from its neck to its widest point is suitable for this task. The gradual taper will allow its use in the forming of bangles and any round units too large for the ring mandrel. The thicker glass of a sparkling-wine bottle, will stand up to light planishing with no risk of its breaking; filled with sand, such a bottle will be even stronger. Remove all the labels. The glass, being very smooth, will impart its texture to the inside of the work.

The knife, fork or spoon must be made of stainless steel, with a plain handle and highly polished on one side. The main requirement is that it should have a smooth design without any pattern, sharp corners or edges which may damage the work during burnishing.

An old screwdriver, rounded off and polished, also makes a good burnisher, especially for use on edges. It has the advantage that it has a comfortable handle. Some of the best burnishers were made of agate.

The burnisher is not a difficult tool to control, but the bigger it is the less risk there is of its slipping off the work and, perhaps, creating an unwanted mark. Where possible, hold the work in a vice and, using both hands, either side of the work, as in draw-filing (see p.31).

The choker made in this way is open at the back, with no hooks or other fastenings, allowing for different pendants to be threaded onto it. To be

TIP THE PROCESS OF BURNISHING NOT ONLY POLISHES BUT ALSO HARDENS THE METAL; THIS CAN BE VERY USEFUL TO THE JEWELLERY MAKER.

YOU WILL NEED:

♦ Sparkling wine bottle

♦ Stainless steel spoon with smooth handle

♦ 2 mm (B&S 12) silver wire, 350 mm (13¾ in.) long.

A sparkling wine bottle and spoon handle can be used to make a choker.

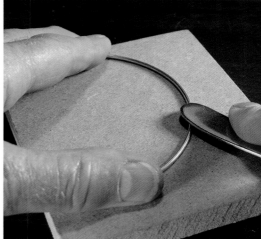

Burnish the outside of the wire while it is wrapped around the bottle, then the top and bottom while it is resting on a flat surface.

secure in use when worn, the wire used must be at least 2 mm thick (B&S 12) and made hard and springy by burnishing. This process will also impart a durable polish to the metal, help it to keep its shape, and make it more resistant to wear.

The length of wire required will depend on the wearer's neck. Make a model in copper wire, if that is possible, but 350 mm (13¾ in.) is about the average length of wire needed for a choker.

In the putting on and removing of this choker, the ends will necessarily rub quite firmly against the wearer's neck. To make it comfortable, make each end round, perfectly smooth and polished. Wrap the wire tightly around the bottle and begin rubbing it firmly with the burnisher. Try to cover the entire surface, which will appear shiny where the burnisher has been applied.

The choker can now be opened out to the correct size by pulling the two ends apart; the roundness will be preserved. With the work resting on a flat, smooth surface, burnish the top and bottom of the piece, turning it over repeatedly. Give it a final polish with rouge applied with a cloth (not with the polishing machine).

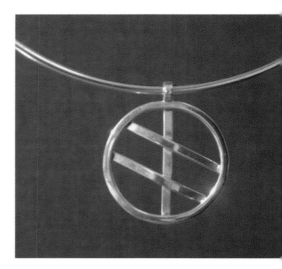

The finished choker can be worn with interchangeable pendants.

4 Punch and die

THE PUNCH AND DIE CONSISTS OF A STEEL ROD, with an angled flat ground at one end, the punch, and a piece of steel with a hole of the same size, the die. To ensure that the punch lines up properly with the hole in the die, you need to create a guide. This usually takes the form of another piece of metal mounted on top of the die to create a kind of sandwich, with the work piece providing the filling. The punch and die works by a shearing action, like a pair of scissors.

There are many advantages to a punched hole when compared with a drilled hole. In the first place, the punch and die creates a disc of waste metal, which can be useful, particularly if it is a precious metal. In fact, the disc may itself be the object of the exercise, and the metal around the hole, the waste. The waste produced by the drilling process is swarf, good for nothing but melting down, if it can be reclaimed at all.

The hole produced by a punch and die is much neater than a drilled hole, without the untidy burr created by the drill. There is a limit to the size of a drilled hole, beyond which it becomes distorted. The greater force required to drill large holes in a thin sheet of metal can lead to accidents as the drill jams in the hole. A piercing saw can be used to create larger holes, but this method requires greater skill and may be less accurate. A punched hole, on the other hand, can be as large as 20 mm (¾ in.), although this size does require a big hammer.

The punch and die.

With the use of a punch and die, holes can overlap each other to allow the creation of elongated holes, whereas a drill, started too close to an existing hole, will always slide into the original hole. The punch and die lends itself very well to the creation of lots of identical units in a given project, with a die being made specifically for that one project. Once made it will last for a good many holes, will save a great deal of time, and will often lead to ideas for projects which may not otherwise be thought of.

MAKING A PUNCH AND DIE

The commercially made punch and die used by professional silversmiths is made to a high standard, hardened and tempered, and built to last. With its extensive range of punches, many of which may not be needed by the amateur, this tool does not come cheap. A rewarding and viable option for the part-time jewellery maker is to make your own, and only requires the use of basic hand tools.

A homemade punch and die will enable the creation of several specific projects, but can be added to and modified to serve other needs as required. Robust enough to withstand the infrequent use it will be subjected to, it may well be a valuable addition to the jewellery maker's toolkit.

Small punches (less than 5 mm in diameter) should be about 25 mm (1 in.) long; if made too long, they are liable to bend, which would of course be disastrous. Larger-sized punches, with little risk of bending, should be about 50 mm (2 in.) long.

TIP PUNCHES MUST ALWAYS BE KEPT SHARP, SO THERE MUST BE ENOUGH LENGTH FOR REPEATED SHARPENING. WHEN A PUNCH BECOMES TOO SHORT IT CAN BE AWKWARD TO USE, AND COULD DAMAGE THE DIE.

The business end of the punch can be ground to an angle, or to a kind of U-shape with two cutting edges, using the corner of the grindstone. The opposite end of the punches should be ground to a chamfer to prevent the swelling or mushroom effect caused by repeated hammering. The chamfer will also clearly distinguish one end of the punch from the other, and thereby prevent mistaken use of the wrong end. It is also useful to make several short lengths of steel rod, chamfered at both ends, for use as guide pins.

Note that the precise thickness of the steel block is not important, but the metal must be thick enough to prevent it bending, and to provide enough length of thread to allow it to be bolted to the top half of the die. This top

A die made from blocks of acrylic and steel, bolted together, and a punched copper sheet.

Remove the burr with a file resting against the side of the punch.

The cutting edge of a punch can be made using the corner of a grindstone.

section also needs to be fairly thick so that the punch is supported square to the hole in the die. This part can be made of metal, though clear acrylic can also be used and this has the advantage of allowing the work to be seen in position. Acrylic is easy to work with and, since there is not much stress on this part of the die, should be strong enough. However, if it should be damaged by accident it can be easily replaced. Make this part of the die a little wider than the base to reduce the risk of it cracking.

A selection of punches.

Guide pins, made from short lengths of steel rod, chamfered at both ends, are very useful.

1. Fix together the two halves of the die using two M6 bolts. Drill both ends of the steel base with 5.5 mm holes and one end of the acrylic block with a 6 mm (¼ in.) hole. Cut the thread in one of the holes with an M6 tap and fix the two halves together with a 25 mm (1 in.) bolt. Drill the second hole in the top using the hole in the steel base as a guide.

2. Cut the thread in the remaining hole in the base. Drill out the hole in the acrylic top to 6 mm (¼in.). If the use of a tap is not available the holes can all be drilled to 6 mm (¼ in.) and the bolts secured with nuts. This will be slightly less convenient in use, whereas cutting threads in the base makes a more positive join and alignment of the holes is more certain.

3. The pattern of holes can now be marked out on the base and drilled. Accuracy is important, so use sharp tools under a good light. Drill the base first. Then, with the two halves bolted together, turn the die over and drill the holes in the top using the bottom half as a guide.

4. Countersink the holes in the top slightly to make it easier to insert the punches. The underside of the die can be drilled out with a slightly larger drill to about half its depth. This makes it easier to remove the waste without the use of excessive force.

> **YOU WILL NEED:**
>
> ◆ Mild steel block, approx. 100 x 25 x 12 mm (4 x 1 x ½ in.)
> ◆ Clear acrylic block, slightly wider than the steel block (or if preferred, a second block of mild steel)
> ◆ M6 tap
> ◆ Two 25 mm (1 in.) M6 bolts

TIP   A BLOCK OF WOOD WITH A HOLE OF ABOUT 25 MM (1 IN.) IN DIAMETER SHOULD BE USED UNDER THE DIE TO ALLOW THE PUNCHES AND WASTE METAL TO DROP THROUGH AND BE RETRIEVED WITHOUT DAMAGE TO THE BENCH.

1

CUFFLINKS

This pair of cufflinks consists of four punched discs, which have been slightly domed and are connected with short lengths of chain. The discs have been embossed with a fabric pattern using the rolling mill. The rolling process has stretched the discs into a slight ellipse to make them more secure in the cuff. The punch and die is the ideal tool for the creation of four identical units such as these.

1. With a permanent pen, draw a line down each side of the silver strip about 1 mm from the edge. This shaded edge will enable the work to be positioned exactly along the centre of the hole in the die (see p.47). With the strip of silver correctly positioned in the die it should be possible to see equal amounts of ink down each side of the 12 mm (½ in.) hole.

2. As each disc is punched out, apply a strip of ink along the cut edge, so that the next disc is created with as little waste as possible. Anneal all four discs and set the rolling mill to slightly thinner than the thickness of the silver. This, together with the fabric, will stretch the metal to about 14 or 15 mm (⅝ in.) long.

3. If a rolling mill is not available, use a cross-peen hammer to create a bark-like effect (see p.24). The cross-peen hammer will have the same effect as the rolling mill, stretching the metal at right angles to the axis of the tool, thereby creating an ellipse. Finish the edges by gripping each between finger and thumb and, holding them vertically, wipe the edges on an emery board.

4. Dome each disc slightly using a dome about 25 mm (1 in.) in diameter. To join the two pairs together, use the method used in the cufflinks with garnets project in the Alternative Methods of Soldering chapter (pp.62).

OXIDISING

The example shown above has been heavily oxidised to create an antique effect. Liver of sulphur is used for this process; a few drops in water will make a strong-enough solution into which to immerse the silver until the preferred colour is achieved. Rock sulphur, used for the treatment of dogs' feet and sold in pet shops, makes a more readily obtainable substitute. Warmed gently in a closed container over a camping stove with the silver, the rock sulphur will turn the metal black. Be warned: the smell is terrible.

YOU WILL NEED:

- 1 mm (B&S 18) silver sheet, 13 x 60 mm (½ x 2¼ in.)
- Material for making links (see p.62)
- Punch and die (see pp.48)

TIP IT IS A GOOD IDEA TO HAVE A MODEL IN COPPER BEING MADE ALONGSIDE THE SILVER ONE SO THAT THE SETTING OF THE ROLLING MILL CAN BE TESTED.

SILVER CHAIN BRACELET

Each 10 mm (³/₈ in.) disc in this bracelet is joined to the 16 mm (⁵/₈ in.) square by a small jump ring, and both units are domed slightly.

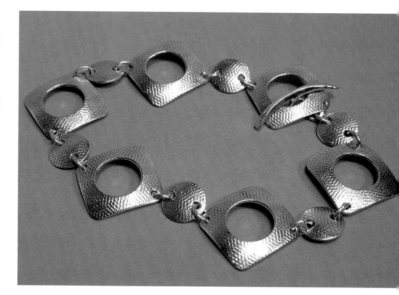

> **YOU WILL NEED:**
>
> ◆ 0.8 mm (B&S 20) silver sheet, 16 x 105 mm (⁵/₈ x 4¹/₈ in.)
>
> ◆ Jump rings made from 1 mm (B&S 18) wire (see pp.109–10 for how to make jump rings, and p.113 for how to calculate the diameter required)
>
> ◆ T-bar (see pp.122–3)
>
> ◆ Punch and die of 10 mm (³/₈ in.) diameter

Use the same method to position the metal in the die as for the cufflinks, but this time the lines are further from the edge, and are also drawn across the metal to indicate the correct position of the holes along the strip (see picture, right). Six squares and six discs, connected with the smallest possible jump rings, and fastened using a forged T-bar (see pp.122–3) located in the last of the punched holes, make a bracelet of approximately 200 mm (8 in.) long.

1. Begin by creating the surface pattern on the metal, then punch out the holes.

2. Cut the squares to length, then round off the corners. To make each square identical, snip off each corner with end cutters, then holding each side against an emery board, wipe each one a given number of times, tilting into the corners.

3. Drill the 1.5 mm (¹/₁₆ in.) holes, as a hole of this size is too small for punching. Holding discs of this size is difficult, so here the wooden hand vice (see pp.32–3) is useful; it can be tightened sufficiently to hold the work securely, but being made of wood will not mark the surface of the metal.

4. Polish the links separately before assembly, threading them onto a piece of thin wire to make holding easier.

PUNCH AND DIE MODEL

Perhaps the most important stage in the process of designing is the modelling stage. A much clearer idea of how a project will look can be gained from a model than can be seen from drawings. Holding something in the hand, even if it is made of card, copper or brass, can give some indication of its scale, and of how it will feel in use.

Making a model of a punch and die is particularly useful. This allows ideas to be formed and tested in ways that might otherwise never be possible.

The proof of this can be seen in the four-hole cross pictured above right. The original idea was to make a cross by punching a hole in each of the four corners of a square. Creating a model showed that the size of the square, and therefore the distance between the holes, made a crucial difference to the appearance of the cross. Making the outside circular, and trimming the sharp corners to a greater or lesser extent, also made a difference. Changing the orientation of the holes to create a completely different style of cross opened up possibilities that only modelling could have demonstrated.

To make this model, drill 4 mm (¹⁄₈ in.) holes at each corner of the two pieces of acrylic, inserting a bolt as each is drilled to make sure that they are correctly aligned. All the holes must be at least 12 mm (½ in.) from the edge of the acrylic to avoid the possibility of its cracking. Drill the holes as required, either singly or in groups.

YOU WILL NEED:

- Two blocks of acrylic,
  100 x 100 x 6 mm (4 x 4 x ¼ in.)
- Four M4 nuts and bolts
- Eight washers

TIP WHEN MAKING THINGS IN ACRYLIC WASHERS ON BOTH SIDES OF THE MATERIAL WILL SPREAD THE LOAD OF THE NUT AND BOLT.

2. The punches used on the model can be the same as those used on the actual punch and die. Alternatively, use any round rod, provided it has a sharp edge ground on its end. A plastic rod, such as a knitting needle, will punch holes in thin card. The main requirement for a punch, both on a model and on the real thing, is that it must be a precise fit in the die. Holes as small as 2 mm can be punched in card, while the minimum size which can be used on metal is probably 3 mm ($^1/_8$ in.).

DOG-TAG CROSS

One of the benefits of making a punch and die, or any jig or former, is that one project can lead to others. Here, two very different crosses have been made using the same combination of holes in the die. The first example has the outline of a US services dog tag, making a pendant with a strong masculine form.

> **YOU WILL NEED:**
>
> ◆ 0.8 mm (B&S 20) silver or bronze sheet, slightly larger than the finished size of 33 x 23 mm (1¼ x $^7/_8$ in.), to allow for error and trimming
>
> ◆ Punch and die (see pp.48–9)

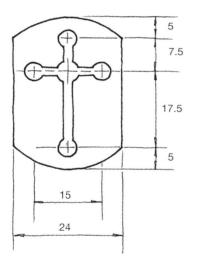

Measurements for dog-tag cross.
All dimensions are in mm.

1. Begin with a piece of 0.8 mm (B&S 20) silver or bronze. Punch the 4 and 5 mm ($^1/_8$ and ¼ in.) holes according to the diagram above. The slots can be sawn out with a piercing saw, but the neatest way is to chisel them out.

The dog-tag cross (RIGHT), and the Cross of Lorraine (LEFT).

2. To chisel them out, make a sandwich of two mild steel bars with a strip of metal 2 mm thick (B&S 12) between them. Bolt them together using M6 bolts with a pin alongside each bolt to prevent the end pieces twisting. Alternatively, use two bolts at either end.

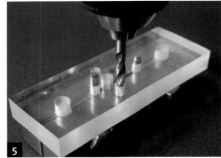

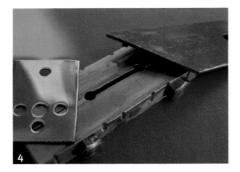

3. Drill two 4 mm holes exactly on the centre line and the same distance apart as the top and bottom holes on the cross.

4. Release the four nuts slightly to allow the middle part of the sandwich to be removed. This will create a slot with a hole at each end.

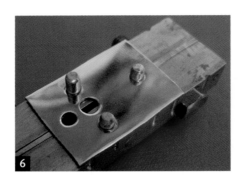

5. Drill the remaining two holes using the acrylic top half of the die as a guide, with a peg in each of the the top and bottom holes.

6. To cut out the vertical slot, hold the work in position using three pegs.

7. The chisel can be made from a strip of mild steel, or as in the example pictured, a piece of broken machine hacksaw blade, cut at an acute angle and ground to a sharp square edge.

8. The horizontal slot, being so short, is probably best sawn out with a piercing saw. All of the slots can, of course, be sawn out; much will depend on how many crosses are to be made.

9. For the finished outline, draw around a template pegged to the work. Then, planish the surface, taking particular care around the slot and the holes to avoid distorting them.

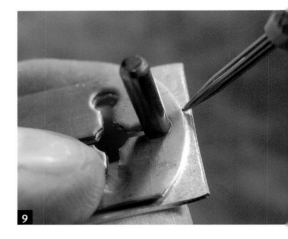

CROSS OF LORRAINE

In the previous project, the cross shape is removed as waste to create a negative shape, leaving no internal corners. When the cross itself is the positive shape, and the metal around it is removed as waste, internal corners are created, making the work more demanding. Cutting into each corner with precision, either with shears or with a saw, is difficult and errors show up quite clearly. Finishing or adjusting each corner with a file can easily make one corner correct at the expense of the others.

YOU WILL NEED:

◆ 0.8 mm (B&S 20) silver or bronze sheet, 45 x 35 mm (1¾ x 1⅜ in.)

◆ Punch and die with punches and pegs

◆ 8 mm diameter ball bearing

When a cross has more than four internal corners, such as on this Cross of Lorraine, the problems are increased. Punching a hole in each corner and then cutting into each one with shears makes the task easier, and the same die holes used on the previous project are used on this one.

1. Begin with a piece of silver or bronze sheet. The two sides are used as reference points when punching the holes, so the width of the blank will determine the proportions of the centre section to the sides. Drill two holes in the die to take pegs to form a fence.

2. Make a mark with a permanent pen where the first hole is to be, and punch the first three holes. To make sure that both sets of vertical holes line up with each other, scribe parallel lines on the underside of the acrylic section of the die. Using a scriber or dividers, make the lines touching the top and bottom of one of the holes; the scribed line will show up quite clearly on any material being punched.

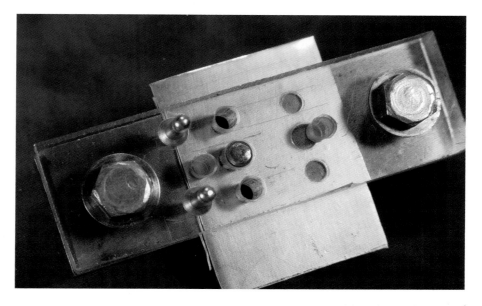

A silver blank clamped in the punch and die. Note the two rivets that are used as a guide along the left edge of the blank. These are used to ensure that both sets of holes are an equal distance from either edge. The scribed line on the underside of the acrylic shows that the holes are in line.

3. Finish the holes by hammering a ball bearing into each one to create a neat countersink.

4. Scribe lines through the centres of all the holes to mark the outline of the cross. It should now be fairly straightforward to cut into each corner with shears, there being little risk of the shears damaging the far sides of the holes.

5. To avoid the narrow sides of the cross becoming distorted, the planishing of this project is best done before the cutting-out stage, leaving only the edges to be slightly bevelled at the end. Punch a 4 mm hole in the top for hanging.

TIP   TO AVOID THE NARROW SIDES OF THE CROSS BECOMING DISTORTED, THE PLANISHING OF THIS PROJECT IS BEST DONE BEFORE THE CUTTING-OUT STAGE, LEAVING THE EDGES TO BE SLIGHTLY BEVELLED AT THE END.

TREFOIL EARRINGS

This pair of earrings, with trefoil cut-outs and hanging beads, could hardly have been made without a punch and die. The punching process has produced distinctive shield-like shapes from which the main units hang. This extra link allows the disc beneath to swing freely, showing off the hammered finish on the slightly domed silver. The discs are 29 mm (1¹/₈ in.) in diameter and the punch is 10 mm (³/₈ in.) in diameter.

The exact shape of the trefoil cut-out is determined by the diameter of the disc, and the distance of the punched holes from the edge of the disc (see drawing, right). The positioning of the large holes, and of the little connecting holes, is best determined by trial and error. In this project more than most others, you are well advised to make a model.

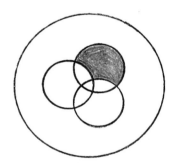

The shaded area – the waste created when the final hole is punched – forms the distinctive shape at the top of the earring.

1. Begin by annealing the 30 mm (1¹/₈ in.) square pieces of metal, which will make cutting out the circles, punching the holes, and hollowing and planishing the silver much easier.

2. Draw out the circle using dividers, or a scriber and a template, which will give a fine line to cut along.

3. Cut off the four corners to just short of the scribed line. Hold the work facing the light, to enable the line to be more clearly seen. When cutting off the bulk of the waste in this way it is important not to cut right up to the line. The remaining metal can then be removed in one continuous piece, leaving a neat square edge. Removing the waste in short lengths and having to restart the cut several times, will be more difficult and will leave a less tidy edge.

The alternatives to this method of cutting out a circle are to cut just short of the line and then finish with a file, which takes much longer, or to use a piercing saw, which requires more skill. Each method should be tried so that a proper judgement can be made as to their relative merits.

4. Smooth the edges with emery boards while the work is still flat and can be held in the vice, or with your fingers.

5. The punching of the holes must also be carried out while the work is still flat. The die has two little holes drilled either side of the 10 mm (³/₈ in.) hole. Pegs are inserted into these, which the edges of the discs rest against, ensuring that all three holes are the same distance from the edge of the disc. Mark three points on the outside of the disc, equidistant from each other. As each hole is punched, one of these points must line up with a reference point on the die; for example, against one of the two pegs. Collect all the punched-out pieces, the last of which will be the shield shape that hangs above the main disc. Drill all the holes for the jump rings 1.5 mm.

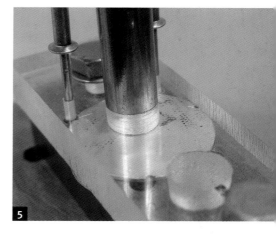

5

The peg lines up with the three points marked on the edge of the disc.

. . . .

TIP   THE METAL MUST BE HELD FIRMLY BETWEEN THE TWO HALVES OF THE DIE TO ENSURE THAT THE METAL REMAINS FLAT AFTER PUNCHING.

. . . .

7. Hollow the discs and the little shields in the largest dome on the doming block, using a wooden punch. Planishing can be either completely random, or the hammer marks can have a circular pattern. It is important to cover the entire surface with hammer marks and ensure that each hammer blow falls on the point of contact between work piece and stake. Any gaps between the work and the stake will result in distortion of the work when the hammer falls on it. The edge of the faces can be finished with a slight bevel by using one side of the hammer face (see pp.28–9). The same bevel can be applied to the edges of the trefoil shapes. Use a burnisher to finish the edges before final polishing with rouge.

8. The bead hangs from a 0.8 mm (B&S 20) wire. The little cup under the bead is a 5 mm (¼ in.) disc punched out of 0.3 mm (B&S 29) sheet and soldered to the end of the wire. Connect all the separate parts with jump rings of 0.8 mm (B&S 20) wire, leaving plenty of room within each ring to allow free movement.

. . . .

TIP   IF THERE ARE SCRATCHES OR OTHER IMPERFECTIONS ON ONE SIDE, THIS SIDE SHOULD BE FACING DOWN IN THE DIE. THIS WILL ENSURE THAT THE SMOOTHEST EDGE IS ON THE FRONT WHERE IT MATTERS MOST.

. . . .

5 Alternative methods of soldering

SUCCESSFUL SOLDERING OFTEN DEPENDS ON the smallest detail. The next few pages are concerned with some alternative solutions to the many and varied problems presented by the process. These include the making of some simple tools and devices.

MAKING AND USING A TURNTABLE

It is often useful to be able to direct the heat from different directions during a soldering operation. Doing this smoothly and rapidly without dislodging finely balanced parts of the work, and maintaining the temperature of the work at or near the melting point of the solder, sometimes requires the use of a turntable.

> **YOU WILL NEED:**
>
> ♦ Two plywood pieces, about 150 x 150 x 15 mm (6 x 6 x ⅝ in.)
> ♦ Two large washers of the type used to join sheets of roofing material
> ♦ Packet of ball bearings of 6 to 8 mm
> ♦ Large curtain ring and some smaller washers (to create the ball race). The size of the rings and washers is not important provided their combined thickness does not exceed the diameter of the ball bearings
> ♦ M6 nut and bolt

1. Cut holes in the middle of both of the plywood pieces large enough to receive a bolt. Cut the corners off one piece to create an octagon, and then glue or screw the offcuts to the corners of the other piece to make raised corners. These become feet that will create space underneath the base for the nut. They will also make for a steadier base. The octagonal top turns more smoothly than a square one.

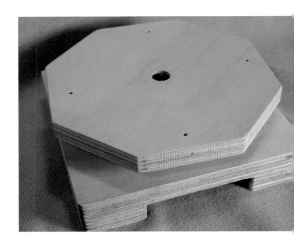

2. A turntable should be able to spin freely, so for this reason a simple bearing is used. Use two large washers for the top and bottom; assembly is more easily carried out with the work upside down. The bolt should have a countersunk head or the wood should be drilled out to bury the head, creating a flush surface. A self-locking nut should be used to allow just the right amount of tightness to prevent it coming loose, but must leave enough clearance for free movement of the bearings.

TIP   DRILL HOLES IN THE TOP SO THAT THE HEATING SURFACE CAN BE SECURED TO IT WITH PINS.

SOLDERING WIRE

The turntable is especially useful when soldering together wire units such as scrolls. Changing the direction of the flame quickly can be vital in preventing disaster. When a ring of wire surrounds the work, this must be heated first to bring it up or near to the melting point of the solder. The ends of the wire, particularly the thinner ends of the scrolls, will get hot much more quickly and can be at much greater risk of melting. A ring which has no end will, all things being equal, take longer to reach the required temperature, the more so when, as in the example shown below right, the ring is made of slightly thicker wire.

The bearing partly assembled (top); and fully assembled (centre). The large washer is next to be threaded onto the bolt, followed by the upturned base then the washer and self-locking nut.

Coat each part of the assembly with flux, and then position them all in the centre of the heating surface. Heat the whole thing until the flux settles down into the varnish-like stage. Carefully place the pallions of easy solder across each join so that they touch both sides. Now heat the outside of the ring, turning the work as you do so; the flame should be pointing away from the centre at all times. As the outside gets hot the flame can be directed at each join in turn.

Try to be aware of what is happening to the work beyond the part that is being soldered, switching direction whenever it appears to be overheating. Both sides of each join should, of course, be heated equally for successful soldering. These rapid changes in the direction of the heat would not be possible without the aid of a turntable.

Sometimes it will be necessary to make multiple joints like this in two stages. The work can be cooled, cleaned in the acid pickle, perhaps bent into shape, refluxed, and small amounts of solder can be added. It may sometimes be necessary to move the more vulnerable sections, such as the tapered ends of wire, away from solder joints to protect them from the heat, moving them back when soldering is complete.

GRADED SOLDERS

Whenever more than one soldered join is carried out on the same piece, graded solder must be considered, although it is not always necessary. Silver solder can be bought in five grades, with enamelling grade having the highest melting point, followed in descending order of melting temperature by hard, medium, easy and extra easy.

All the remaining projects in this section involve making settings for cabochons called rub-over settings. Each project will be concluded with the soldering stage, while the actual setting of the cabochons will be explained in a separate section at the end (see pp.65–66).

PENDANT WITH ROLLED BAIL

This pendant with its rolled bail is set with a cabochon. To make the pendant two grades of solder, hard and easy, are used. Hard is used to make the bezel, while easy is used to join the bezel to the base.

Measuring the height that the bezel using dividers against the cabochon. The bezel must be high enough to hold the cabochon securely, but not so high as to obscure it.

YOU WILL NEED:

- 0.3 mm (B&S 29) silver, 3 x 25 mm (¹/₈ x 1 in.). The width of the strip will be the height of the bezel, and will be determined by measuring the cabochon (see picture above).
- Hard and easy solder
- 8 mm round cabochon
- 0.8 mm (B&S 20) silver, cut to a triangle shape, approx. 50 mm (2 in.) long and 20 mm (¾ in.) at the widest end.

FOR THE SUPPORT:

- Two lengths of steel fencing wire (or a wire coat hanger)
- Block of wood, about 125 x 125 mm (5 x 5 in.)
- Piece of fine wire mesh the same size as the wood.

1. Form the strip into a ring and join it using hard solder to form the bezel that holds the cabochon. The join is best done with the work on its side; use a bent nail to prevent it falling over. The thickness of bezel material is a compromise: too thin will make for more difficult and risky soldering, but too thick may make it difficult to push over onto the cabochon.

2. Make the bezel round on a small tapered mandrel, gently tapping it until it has stretched enough to fit the cabochon. This should be a loose fit: when the bezel is placed over the stone you should be able to lift it clear without picking up the cabochon. Flatten the top and bottom by rubbing on an emery board, using a fingertip to prevent any distortion.

TIP CHECK THE BEZEL AGAINST THE CABOCHON BEFORE SOLDERING IT TO THE BASE. IT SHOULD BE A LOOSE FIT ON THE CABOCHON.

3. Mix the flux slightly thicker than usual, dip the bezel into the flux and place it in position on the base using tweezers. Leave it to rest for a few moments, then lift it clear to leave a circular imprint of flux. It may be necessary to carry out this routine several times, cleaning the base between each attempt before a neat circular imprint of flux is created. Remix the flux to its proper milk-like consistency and wash off the thick coating of flux from the bezel.

4. Place five tiny pallions of easy solder around the ring of flux, and then carefully balance the bezel on top of them. This delicate operation is best done with both hands resting on the bench, and with the tweezers held like a pen.

TIP FIVE SMALLER PALLIONS ARE PREFERRED TO THREE OR FOUR LARGER ONES. THIS ENSURES THAT THE SOLDER IS RESTRICTED TO THE NARROW AREA UNDER THE BEZEL. A LARGE PALLION WILL SOMETIMES LEAVE A TINY MARK OR PRINT WHICH WILL HAVE TO BE FILED AWAY.

5. The next stage must be carried out with the work supported at a height and heated from underneath. The support is made from two lengths of steel fencing wire bent into shape in a vice. A wire coat hanger can also be used. Drill four holes in a piece of wood for the base and push the ends into them. place a piece of wire mesh on the top. The mesh should be as fine as possible; this one came from a disposable barbecue. When not in use, the support can be taken apart for ease of storage.

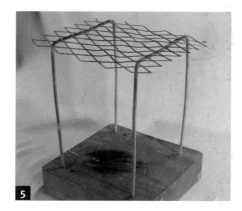

6. To complete the soldering it only remains to place the work carefully onto the mesh and heat it to the required temperature. The piece should be evenly heated so that all the pallions melt simultaneously. By heating it from underneath in this way, the larger base heats up without the tiny bezel being exposed to the heat. If the work were to be heated from above, the bezel would overheat and probably melt, long before the base became hot enough to melt the solder. The original joint on the bezel, having been made with hard solder, is unlikely to re-melt during the second soldering operation.

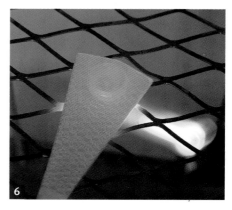

CUFFLINKS WITH GARNETS

The making of these cufflinks will require that the work be heated three times, but only two grades of solder will be used.

YOU WILL NEED:

♦ Easy and hard solder

♦ Two matching oval cabochons, approx. 10 mm (³⁄₈ in.) long by 8 mm wide

♦ 0.8 mm (B&S 20) silver sheet, cut into two identical rectangular base pieces, on which to mount the cabochons, 16 x 14 mm (⁵⁄₈ x ½ in.)

♦ 0.3 mm (B&S 29) silver wire for the bezels (see step 2 for how to calculate the length required)

♦ Two short pieces of 1 mm wire

1. Melt two pallions of easy solder onto the middle of the back of the base to form a small pool of solder. This solder will be melted more than once but will be none the worse for that, provided flux is used each time.

2. To calculate the length of metal needed for the bezel, add the length of the oval cabochon to the width, and divide this dimension by two. Multiply this figure by pi (3.14), which is the circumference of the stone. It is better to underestimate this dimension than to make it too long. It is much easier to stretch a bezel by planishing than to cut out and rejoin it to make it smaller. Make the bezel using hard solder for the join.

3. When the bezel is an easy fit around the cabochon, it must be soldered to the base. Make a flux imprint as in the pendant with rolled bail project (p.60), place six pallions for the bezel to rest on, and solder it in place.

4. The setting must be heated from underneath. If not using the support described for the pendant project (see pp.60–1), an alternative method, and one more appropriate for small items, is to hold the work in locked tweezers. A steel washer is used for this purpose; this one has a flat edge filed on one side to prevent it rolling sideways. The work can now be balanced on the edge of the bench and heated from below. The little pool of solder underneath must be coated with flux so that, when it re-melts, it will remain smooth, and none will be lost as oxide.

4a

4b

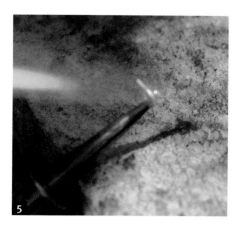

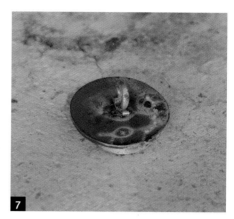

5. A link must now be soldered to the back, to which a chain will be attached. To make this link, wind a piece of 1 mm wire around a 2-inch nail or similar and snip off the ends so that they lie side by side. Join using easy solder.

6. Replace the link on the nail, and hammer the overlapping section to create a flat area that will balance on the upturned setting.

7. The final soldering join can now be carried out, with the work resting upside down on a flat surface. Flux both sides of the work and place the link on top of the little pool of solder. Direct the flame to the area around the link as this will take longer to heat. As the solder on both pieces re-melts, the link will settle into place. The solder on the bezel underneath the work will probably re-melt, but not to the detriment of the join.

How to make the 'T' bar is shown on p.122. This is joined to the front of the link by a short length of chain connected by jump rings. The distance between front and back of a pair of cufflinks should be about 20 mm (¾ in.)

TIP   THE PROCESS WHEREBY SOLDER IS MELTED ONTO BOTH SIDES OF A JOIN SEPARATELY, AND THEN RE-MELTED TOGETHER, IS CALLED SWEATING. THIS TECHNIQUE IS OFTEN APPROPRIATE WHEN SMALL DELICATE COMPONENTS ARE TO BE JOINED.

SET OF THREE RINGS

The making of this set of rings presents a soldering problem for which there is more than one solution. It is important that the three rings are the same size, so cut the three blanks of 1.5 mm (B&S 15) wire to exactly the same length, in this example 60 mm (2³/₈ in.), which makes a ring of UK size Q.

YOU WILL NEED:

◆ 1.5 mm (B&S 15) silver wire, cut into three equal lengths according to the desired ring size (see table on p.140)

◆ Three cabochons

◆ 0.25 mm (B&S 30) silver sheet, cut into three 19 mm lengths (for the width, measure the cabochon height; see p.60)

◆ 0.5 mm thick (B&S 24) silver sheet, 9 x 40 mm

1. Join all three ring blanks using easy solder. Make them round using a mallet to ensure that they are not made larger.

2. Flatten each ring using a flattening device or with a hammer on a flat stake. The thickness is not important, it only matters that each ring is the same thickness all round and that all three are identical. Before this process goes too far, make a slight mark with the edge of a file where the join is, . Finish each face on an emery board to make sure they are flat and clean.

3. The bezels are made from a 19 mm silver strip joined with hard solder. Solder each bezel to the end of the strip of silver, using locked tweezers to hold the strip. Trim off the majority of the waste with shears, then nibble most of what remains with end cutters, leaving a small ridge to be filed off after it is joined to the ring.

4. To join the settings to the rings, begin by melting a pallion of easy solder to the underside of each setting. To ensure that the ring is positioned in the middle of the setting, arrange the work on its side. The ring rests on part of a large paperclip, one end of which has been bent up to form a sloping platform. With the setting resting against a ceramic block, the ring can be positioned at the correct height by moving it up or down the slope.

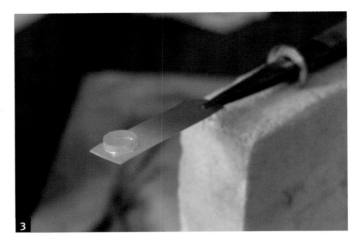

5. It is usually best to join the setting to that part of the ring furthest from the original join. A pallion of easy solder should be placed on the ring, touching the pool of solder on the setting. An alternative method for holding this work is to balance the ring on the upturned setting held in place with locked tweezers.

6. The final truing up of the setting is done after it is joined to the ring.

Hold the ring in a wooden vice for final finishing.

SETTING A CABOCHON

When soldering is complete, and the work has been thoroughly cleaned in the acid pickle to remove every bit of spent flux, the next stage is the setting of the cabochon. The polishing stage is best left until after the stone is in place, as polishing can sometimes wear down the thin metal of the bezel if it is left exposed.

If the cabochon is translucent, or even if it is not completely opaque, the ground under the stone should be brightened to show off the stone to its best effect. This is best done with a scraper such as a penknife. No attempt should be made to polish the surface; the scraped surface alone creates a brighter ground.

Make sure there are no filings or dirt in the setting, and check that the bezel is the correct height by placing the cabochon alongside it. Scrape off any burr from the edge of the bezel. Only when you are completely satisfied that all is correct should the stone be inserted. It is easy to have the cabochon stick in the setting before it has been properly prepared, and it can be difficult to get out.

In stone-setting, the work must be held securely so that it doesn't slip. The holding device must also be tough enough to withstand the substantial force required to push the bezel over the stone. A golfer's tee peg is a suitable support to push against, and being made of plastic, will not harm the edge of the metal. The peg can be inserted into a block of wood drilled with holes, and this device will be easier to hold than the work itself.

The pusher is made from a 3 mm (1/8 in.) mild steel rod set in a wooden handle. The size of the pusher is important: too large and it can be difficult to force the metal over, but too small and it is likely to damage the thin silver. The end should be smooth but not polished, which would make it more likely to slip.

Slips are likely during this process due to the force applied and considerable damage can be caused to the surface of the work. This damage can be difficult to remove from a textured surface. For this reason, it is worth your while to make a protective cover. Use a soft metal such as copper, punch a hole in it and roll it out until it fits over the bezel. Anneal it and smooth off all the edges.

Check the height of the bezel by laying the cabochon alongside it.

Scrape the surface of the setting where the cabochon will sit.

A golf tee makes a suitable support against which to push the bezel on to the cabochon.

The pusher should be held at an angle of 45 degrees and applied to the top edge of the bezel. The pusher is held between forefinger and thumb with the handle against the palm of the hand, which is where the force is applied.

Place the stone in the bezel. Begin by pushing down the four opposing sides of the bezel; this will ensure that the cab is not pushed to one side in the setting. Continue pushing the bezel down onto the cabochon until no gaps remain between stone and bezel. When all the bumps and ridges have been flattened against the stone, use a burnisher to finish the top edge.

The highly polished tool is forced against the top edge of the bezel, a small section at a time, to create a hard, polished edge and a tight seal between the stone and the metal. The protective cover should be in place throughout this process, to allow force to be applied without risk of damage to the surrounding metal.

A close examination of the setting may reveal some lumps or imperfections in the solder join. These can be smoothed out with a Water of Ayr stone, the end of which has been ground to an angle. Work on small sections at a time, and keep the stone in the angle between the base and the bezel to ensure that only this limited area is touched by the stone.

The Water of Ayr stone creates a smooth, pre-polish surface which can now be finished off on the corner of the polishing machine and with polishing pads. It is easy to create streaks on the base around the setting. To avoid this, the work must be moved around constantly to prevent the polisher from resting on any one section at a time.

....

TIP   WHEN SETTING THE CABOCHONS THE CUFFLINKS AND THE RINGS SHOULD BE HELD IN THE WOODEN HAND VICE. THE WORK SHOULD BE SUPPORTED AGAINST THE BENCH PEG IN THE SAME WAY THAT THE PENDANT IS HELD AGAINST THE TEE PEGS (SEE PICTURE 10 ON P.80).

....

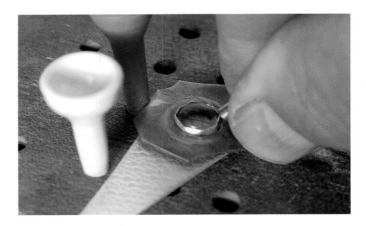

Pushing the bezel against the stone with the protective cover in place.

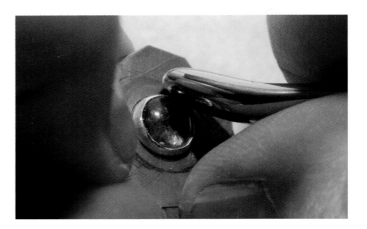

Creating a polished edge with a burnisher. The protective cover protects the surrounding metal.

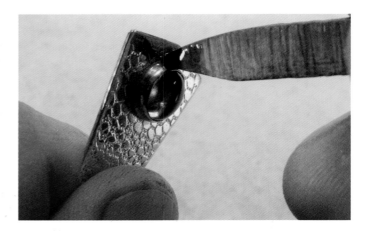

Smoothing the corner between the base and the bezel with Water of Ayr stone.

6 Wire scroll work

OF ALL THE FORMS OF METAL AVAILABLE TO THE JEWELLERY maker, wire is perhaps the most useful and the least troublesome to work with. Wire is obtainable in all sizes and many different sections: round, half-round, square, oval and flat. Wire can be twisted on itself, or with other wires, and bending with pliers or in a jig is not difficult. It is possible, and sometimes desirable, to bend wire using just fingers and thumbs, nowhere more so than in scroll work.

Bending wire into scroll forms, then joining these to make a design, offers countless possibilities. The separate pieces can be joined together in different ways, and the negative shapes between the wire units give a Celtic flavour to the designs. Placing one or more scrolls within a circular border adds to the Celtic effect, as well as providing a hanging or fixing device.

Some of the many varied scroll forms that can be used in jewellery making.

CELTIC BROOCH

For the first of the designs a single 'S' scroll is mounted within a circular ring and used with a pin to make a brooch.

> **YOU WILL NEED:**
>
> ♦ 1.3 mm (B&S 16) silver wire, cut into two lengths of 80 mm (3¹/₈ in.)
>
> ♦ 1.5 mm (B&S 15) silver wire, 80 mm (3¹/₈ in.) long

1. Form the thicker length of wire into a ring and make it round on a mandrel. Use a mallet at this stage as it is important to maintain the round section to the wire until the work is soldered together.

2. Forming scrolls, or at least the difficult starting stage of the process, is made easier when the wire is tapered towards the end. Holding the wire with pliers, or in a hand vice, file a flat section about 10 mm (³/₈ in.) long to about half the thickness of the wire at the tip. This thinner end will bend more easily around the jaw of the round-nosed pliers, and will also improve the appearance of the scroll.

3. The first stage in the forming of a scroll is the most important. Use round-nosed pliers to shape the end of the wire into a half-circle. The round-nosed pliers, which are quite likely to damage the wire, can then be discarded, and parallel pliers, or the ends of flat pliers, can then be used for the remainder of the work.

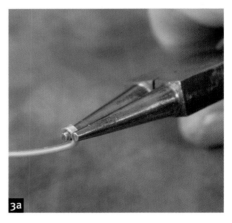

Grip the wire firmly with the parallel or flat pliers at the point where the curve ends and the straight section begins, and pull or bend it with your fingers, watching the gap between the wires to keep the turn of the scroll even. To make a symmetrical S-scroll, stop when the straight section is half the original length of the wire.

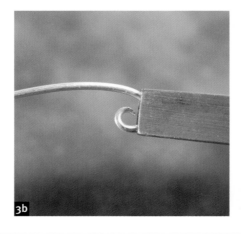

4. Push the finished S-scroll together, or pull it apart with your fingers, until it makes a tight fit in the circular ring.

5. Make the pin by forming a slightly smaller scroll on the remaining piece of wire, then file a point at the other end. Do not attempt to make the point too long and sharp. Harden the pin by gently hammering it while rolling it across a flat stake. This is also the best way to make the pin straight.

6. Solder the S-scroll into the ring, with the scroll sideways onto the flame. Heat the ring first, as this will take longer to heat up. Dome the work slightly then planish it on a slightly curved stake.

GECKO PENDANT

TIP   WHENEVER SCROLLS OR OTHER ROUND WIRE UNITS ARE JOINED, THEY SHOULD BE PLANISHED AFTER THEY HAVE BEEN SOLDERED. SOLDER WILL ALWAYS FLOW MORE READILY INTO THE JUNCTION BETWEEN ROUND WIRES.

YOU WILL NEED:

◆ 1.3 mm (B&S 16) wire, 200 mm (8 in.) long (for the body)

◆ 1.3 mm (B&S 16) wire, cut into two lengths of 100 mm (4 in.) (for the legs)

TIP   IN THIS EXAMPLE A CLOSED SCROLL IS USED. THIS TYPE OF SCROLL REQUIRES A LONGER AND SHARPER TAPER ON THE END OF THE WIRE; THE TIP IS THEN BENT COMPLETELY AROUND ITSELF TO REST AGAINST THE SIDE OF THE WIRE.

1. Bend the wire double, making one side slightly longer than the other, and form a scroll at each end. Make a scroll at each end of the shorter pieces to form the legs.

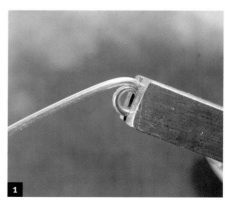

2. When all the scrolls have been formed the pliers can be discarded; it is probably better to use fingers and thumbs to form the curves of the body. When the body is correctly shaped, solder the two sides of the tail together.

3. Attach the legs by holding them in position with fingers on a flat stake and giving the joint a sharp tap with a heavy hammer. This will create a little hollow on each side of the join, which will help to keep it in place during soldering. Solder, then planish the whole piece, concentrating the hammer on some parts of the body more than others, to vary the apparent width of the wire when seen from the front.

TIP   TAKE EXTRA CARE WHEN POLISHING THIS KIND OF PROJECT: IT IS EASY TO TANGLE SCROLL WORK IN THE POLISHING MOP. WORK ON ONE SMALL SECTION AT A TIME AND TAKE NO RISKS. IF THERE IS A PART THAT IS DIFFICULT TO REACH SAFELY, IT MAY BE BETTER TO POLISH THAT SECTION BY HAND.

S-SCROLL PENDANTS

Combining several units in a project adds to the effectiveness of the scroll shapes, exploiting the negative spaces between the wires. The closed scroll, where the pointed end of the wire is wrapped around to lie against the side of the wire to form a complete circle, will usually make more interesting negative shapes between the wires. Here, three identical S-scrolls are combined to make a pendant. The simple hanging device – a pair of jump rings joined to a larger ring fastened to a leather cord – does not detract too much from the main elements of the project.

Three 150 mm (6 in.) lengths of 1.5 mm (B&S 15) wire are used to make the three units. When two or more units are combined in this way, it is often desirable to make them identical. This is especially the case in this project, as the wire has not been planished; planishing can help to disguise small inaccuracies. The creation of identical units can be achieved with practice, but there are also some simple strategies which can be helpful.

The eye is often drawn to the centre of a scroll, so getting this part right is especially important. To ensure

all the scrolls start in the same way, place a tiny wire ring on one jaw of the round-nosed pliers, or mark a point on the jaw with a permanent pen, or use the extreme end of the pliers to help to make each one alike. A tapered pin, such as a knitting needle, which can be pushed through the centre of a closed scroll to a marked point (the circles having originally been made slightly smaller than the required size), will also work. This technique will also help to correct any faults in the work by forcing the ends against the adjacent wire. You can also use the same tapered pin to make adjustments to the scrolls, by pushing it between the coils over a hole in a block of wood.

A guide on one jaw of the pliers will ensure that all the scrolls are the same.

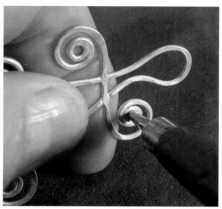

Pushing a tapered pin through the scroll to make adjustments to the centre.

Having achieved an acceptable uniformity in the three scrolls, lay them out against one another to establish the most effective combination. The range of possible combinations is extensive, and even slight changes in the position of one unit relative to another can alter the overall effect markedly. Decide whether there is a preferred front to the project, as soldering is best carried out on the reverse. Finally, bend the vulnerable ends of the scrolls clear of the joins as far as is possible. It will be easy to return them to their former shape after they have been soldered.

Planishing will often improve the look of wire projects, but in this case the crowded scroll work creates an effect on the surface of the metal which would not be improved by this technique. The fact that the work is not planished creates the problem that it will remain soft after the soldering process. However, simply making adjustments will help to harden the work, as will bending it back and forth using your fingers.

Try out different placements of the scrolls to discover the most attractive arrangement.

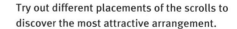

Extra care will be needed during polishing as the softer wire can easily be pulled out of shape by the polishing wheel. Direct the wheel onto limited and tightly held areas, while continually changing the direction of the wheel relative to the work.

This alternative design has been made from 1.3 mm (B&S 16) wire in 120 mm (4¾ in.) lengths. In this case, planishing has been applied to vary the width of the wires when seen from the front. This, combined with the slightly more elongated shape of each unit, creates an altogether different effect.

Slight changes to the shape of each unit, or their relation to each other, make a big difference to the overall effect.

S-SCROLL BRACELET

An S-scroll is not the most stable form, as it is easily pulled out of shape; while the bracelet is perhaps the most vulnerable form of jewellery, often getting caught in clothing. For this bracelet, some reinforcement has been created by using smaller scrolls that tie both ends of each unit together.

This reinforcement creates a closed end to each unit which limits the options for the joining links. If closed links are used these must be threaded on while one end of the main scroll is still straight. The small scrolls will then have to be soldered onto an assembled chain.

An alternative method is to use jump rings. To make them a little more interesting, these are used in sets of three and, being oval, will lie closer to the wrist. By using jump rings, which can be opened and closed, you can completely finish each scroll unit, including planishing, polishing and bending to the required radius, before the units are assembled.

Oval jumprings on an oval nail ready for polishing.

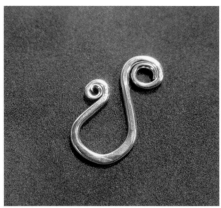

Use trial and error to find the right length for the hook.

The jump rings are made on a 2-inch oval nail (see p.110), which should be about 3.5 mm (¹/₈ in.) wide. When the units are assembled the joins are arranged at the back and, being oval, will remain there. The catch is a simple hook connecting three oval jump rings, which as well as matching the rest of the jump rings, will also add a bit of extra security. The length of the hook is important: too short and it may slip out of the rings; too long and it will be difficult to fasten. You will find the right length through trial and error.

WIRE SCROLL PENDANT AND EARRINGS

Not all scroll projects have a Celtic flavour, and there is no unbreakable rule that all the coils must be evenly spaced. In these examples, precise and regular coils are abandoned for a more random arrangement to create a very different style. The appearance of a random arrangement is deceptive, as these examples have, in fact, been arrived at after much trial and error, and there is a sort of system to their making.

With practice, and the systematic use of round-nosed and parallel pliers, a kind of uniformity can be achieved, to make this pendant with matching earrings. The pendant is made using 1.5 mm (B&S 15) wire, while the earrings are made from 1.2 mm (B&S 17) wire. The pendant wire is 280 mm (11 in.) long and the earrings are 240 mm (9½ in.) long.

It is worth making lots of copper wire models before using silver wire; minor differences in the thickness of the wire used, for example, can have a marked effect on the look of the finished piece. These models will be useful at the soldering and planishing stages of the project. It will be almost impossible to measure the length of wire in a scroll after it has been formed, so when modelling scrolls it is advisable for future reference to measure and make a note of the length of the wire while it is still straight.

Begin by bending the squared-off end of the wire with round-nosed pliers to form an eye. Then, gripping the wire just under the eye, bend it around itself until it touches the eye. Using the eye as a former, and parallel pliers, bend the wire around keeping both wires in line with each other. Continue the bending, using round-nosed pliers for the corners, and parallel pliers to keep the wires in line with each other when they come together.

Finish by forming an eye on the end, making sure that it touches the wire to complete the circle. Solder this join as well as two or three more joins where the wires touch. This will strengthen the piece and make it less likely it will be pulled out of shape. It is not necessary to solder every one of these points.

TIP   ONE OF THE FEW RULES FOR SCROLL DESIGN IS THAT THERE SHOULD BE NO STRAIGHT SECTIONS OF WIRE, WHICH IS WHY FINGERS ARE OFTEN PREFERRED TO PLIERS FOR SOME OF THE WORK.

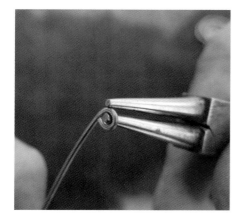

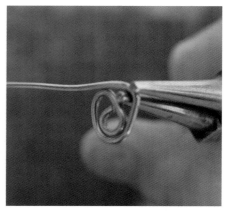

Using parallel pliers keeps the wires in line with each other, but use round-nosed pliers for the corners.

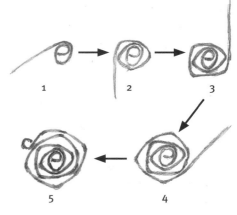

This type of scroll should be planished to show it off to best effect. Direct the hammer to one part more than another, to create a variation in the width of the wire. This stage can make or break the project and may require some practice using the copper models.

TIP   TO HELP TO MAKE EACH UNIT IDENTICAL, THE COPPER WIRE MODELS SHOULD BE PLACED BESIDE THE UNIT BEING WORKED ON, AND CONSTANTLY REFERRED TO DURING EACH STAGE OF THE BENDING AND PLANISHING.

An alternative strategy for making this kind of scroll is to create a jig using nails in plywood. After the first loop has been made, drill a 2 mm hole in the wood and, with the work pinned in place using a nail, drill another hole against the wire just where the round-nosed pliers would be positioned. Continue in this way with a nail hole in the place where the round-nosed pliers would be used. Making a jig of this sort will often be the best way to achieve the uniformity needed in jewellery such as bracelets and necklaces, which are made up of identical units.

The bending sequence. To make all three parts of the project the same check the scroll carefully after making each bend.

Lots of practice with copper wire will inevitably lead to the accumulation of a collection of samples which can be a useful aid in project design. Different thicknesses of wire and methods of planishing should also be tried and compared.

Lots of drawings combined with the making of models in copper wire is the best way to achieve sucessful solutions.

7 The doming block

THE FORMING OF SHEET METAL USING THE DOMING BLOCK is one of the easiest forming processes to master. The creation of hemispheres of a consistent radius from discs of equal size makes it possible to produce matching halves of beads, or sets of identical units, with relative ease.

The most expensive doming blocks are made of steel and provide the greater durability required by the professional jeweller. However, the majority of doming blocks are made of brass; the cheaper ones tend to have fairly shallow domes. The domes in a doming block should ideally be hemispherical. The doming block is used with punches, which can be made of steel or wood. A wooden punch is easy to make, will not damage the doming block, and will form all but the toughest of metals.

TIP   A BALL BEARING STRUCK WITH A HEAVY HAMMER MAKES AN ADEQUATE SUBSTITUTE FOR A METAL PUNCH WHEN THICK METAL IS TO BE DOMED.

The doming block with a wooden punch.

RING WITH A DOMED MOUNT

The surface of a dome formed in a doming block will always be part of a sphere. As a result, the squared-off end of a round tube such as the bezel for a cabochon will always be a perfect fit on such a dome. Here, a domed square of silver is used on a ring as part of the mount for a 10 mm (³/₈ in.) diameter cabochon.

YOU WILL NEED:

- 0.8 mm (B&S 20) silver sheet, 62 x 7 mm (2½ x ⁵/₁₆ in.) (for ring size P)
- 0.8 mm (B&S 20) silver sheet, 15 x 15 mm (⁵/₈ x ⁵/₈ in.), for the base of the mount
- 0.3 mm (B&S 29) silver sheet, 32 mm (1¼ in.) long, for the bezel (the height of the bezel will determine the width required; see p.60)
- 10 mm (³/₈ in.) diameter cabochon
- Hard and easy solder

TIP   To find the right length of metal for a particular ring use the table on p.140. Alternatively, wrap a strip of adhesive paper around the finger and mark where it overlaps. Remember to wrap it around the widest part of the finger, usually the knuckle.

1. Begin by making a ring from the strip of silver. Prepare the joint using the piercing saw as necessary.

2. When soldering, position the ring with the joint uppermost and with the solder placed on the outside surface (see p.26). This area will later be obscured by the dome. Make the ring round on a ring mandrel, and give it a preliminary polish. It will clearly be more difficult to polish the ring after it has been soldered to the setting.

Sawing down an imperfect join with a piercing saw creates a parallel gap which can then be closed up to perfect the join.

3. Take the square piece of silver and make the edges square on an emery board. Place the emery board flat on the bench and hold the work at right angles to it. Draw the metal along the board, tilting it onto its corner as you do so. Do this the same number of times on all four sides, then turn it over and do the same from the other direction. This should make the corners identical. Polish the edges at this stage, while the work is still flat.

4. Dome the little square using successive domes until it is a good fit on the ring. Ensure that the entire surface is covered by the wooden punch, to make it perfectly spherical.

The square of silver with rounded corners is ready for the doming process.

. . . .

TIP ALWAYS CHECK VERY CAREFULLY FOR BITS OF GRIT IN A DOMING BLOCK. A SCRATCH OR A DENT IN A DOMING BLOCK WILL CREATE RIDGES OR LUMPS ON THE WORK WHICH ARE EASILY REMOVED. A PIECE OF GRIT, ON THE OTHER HAND, WILL LEAVE INDENTATIONS IN THE WORK WHICH WILL TAKE A LONG TIME, AND SOME WASTAGE, TO REMOVE. IT WILL ALSO INFLICT SIMILAR INDENTATIONS IN THE DOMING BLOCK, AND THIS DAMAGE, BEING IN A HOLLOW, WILL BE VERY DIFFICULT TO PUT RIGHT.

. . . .

5. The domed square must now be prepared to hold the cabochon. A platform, perfectly flat and in the centre of the dome, must be created for the stone to rest on. To make this task easier, drill a hole in a piece of thin plywood just large enough to contain the dome. Resting the dome in the hole overcomes the problem of how to hold the work. The surface of the plywood provides a guide for the file, and this will ensure that the little platform, roughly 6 mm (¼ in.) in diameter, is in the centre of the domed square and perfectly flat.

As an alternative, an 8 mm hole can be punched in the centre of the square. Positioning a punched hole accurately can be difficult. If the metal is cut slightly over size, it can be trimmed with shears after the hole is punched to ensure that the hole is exactly in the centre of the square.

6. Make a bezel using a strip of 0.3 mm (B&S 29) silver 32 mm (1¼ in.) long. To establish the width required, rest the cabochon on the top of the dome to set the dividers as shown in the diagram, right. It is better to make the bezel too high rather than too low – it can be filed down, but cannot be made higher.

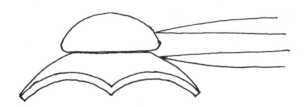

Setting the dividers to the correct height for the bezel.

After soldering with hard solder, stretch the bezel on a mandrel to make it a loose fit around the cabochon. It will not be possible to check the height of the bezel with the cabochon alongside, so the slightly looser fit allows for the placing of the cab inside the bezel with no risk of its sticking.

7. The soldering of the bezel to the dome will, of course, require that the work is heated from underneath. An alternative to the four-legged stand is to use strips of firebrick overhanging the bench with a spacer between, held down by a heavy weight. The six pallions are placed inside the bezel, touching both dome and bezel.

8. The final soldering task is to join the ring to the dome. Flux the previous joins and the inside of the dome and place it on a flat firebrick. Coat the ring with flux and position it on the upturned dome with the join in the centre. Place two pallions of easy solder on either side of the ring, touching both ring and dome. The original solder joins will probably re-melt, but with the work positioned as it is, and all the joins covered with flux, the re-melting will not affect the joins.

9. After a long soak in the acid pickle, the finishing process can be started. The slope of the metal away from the join means that the bezel and the area around it will be easy to make smooth using emery boards. Use Water of Ayr stone to smooth the ring alongside the dome, taking care not to catch the edge of the dome.

10. Set the cabochon as shown on pp.65–6. The setting of the cabochon will be made easier if the ring is held in a vice. This wooden hand vice has been widened to take this ring (picture 9), and with packing pieces can also be used to hold narrower rings. Rest the work with the corner of the bezel against the bench peg to prevent damage to the dome.

DOMED EARRINGS

The doming block is central to the design and making of these earrings. The flat border on the front of the concave discs makes a polished frame around the hollowed, textured and oxidised area. The connections for the hanging bunches of beads are concealed behind the domes. Soldering the connections to the back in this way avoids the necessity of drilling the discs and leaves the framed concave surface unspoiled.

YOU WILL NEED:

- Two 22 mm (⅞ in.) diameter silver discs, punched from 0.8 mm (B&S 20) silver (surface texture should be applied before the discs are cut out)
- Plywood, 100 x 50 x 12 mm (4 x 2 x ½ in.)
- Two one-inch round nails
- 1 mm (B&S 18) round wire, approx. 500 mm (20 in.) long
- Two 8 mm (⁸⁄₁₆ in.) diameter beads
- Four 6 mm (¼ in.) diameter beads
- Two ear wires

TIP   THE SURFACE TEXTURE OF THE DISCS CAN BE CREATED WITH A ROLLING MILL OR PLANISHING HAMMER. TO PREVENT ANY DISTORTION OF THE DISCS BY THE ROLLING MILL OR HAMMER, THE CIRCLES ARE CUT OUT AFTER THE PATTERN IS APPLIED.

1. Place the discs in the doming block, patterned side uppermost, and dome them using a wooden doming punch to prevent any damage to the surface.

2. The connections are made as one unit, which makes it easier to solder them to the domes. A simple jig will make it easier to make them identical. A piece of plywood is drilled with three holes, the centres of which are 7 mm apart. The middle hole is 8 mm and the smaller ones are 2 mm in diameter. the little dowel is 25 mm (1 in.) long, as are the two round nails. There is a 1 mm hole to one side, which is used to secure the end of the wire at the start.

3. To make the connections, wrap 1 mm (B&S 18) silver wire around the pegs as shown on p.81. Solder the wires together where they cross, joining the open end first. Hammer the joins flat, make the large ring completely round on a mandrel and solder the unit to the outside of the dome.

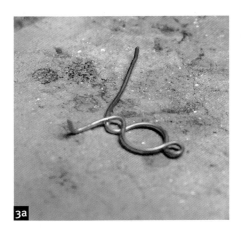

3a

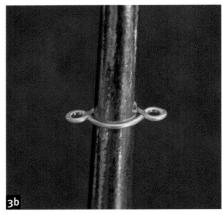

3b

3c

4. Thread a thin piece of wire through the eyes to give you something to hold, and, using a disc sander or a series of emery boards, make the front edge completely flat and smooth. Clean the work thoroughly and oxidise it using liver of sulphur (see p.50). Carefully polish the inside and the back of the dome, preserving some of the oxide, and give the outside edge a final polish on a polishing pad to remove all trace of oxide on this flat surface.

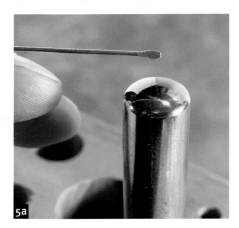

5a

5b

5. The bead hanging wires are made from 1 mm (B&S 18) round wire. The simplest of jigs is used to make them identical. Begin by creating a little fishtail on the end of the wire, trim it, then smooth it with an emery board, then thread on the bead.

6. Drill a 2 mm hole in a piece of plywood and, at a point 35 mm from this hole drill an 8 mm hole. Drill a 6 mm hole at a point 38 mm from the 2 mm hole and push a one-inch nail into the small hole. With one finger holding a bead in its hole, and another holding down the wire, bend the wire around the nail at right angles.

7. Using the width of the jaws of the parallel pliers as a guide to the length, cut off the wire and true-up the end using a smooth file. With the tip of the round-nosed pliers, bend it around to form the eye. To preserve its rounded shape the eye must be opened and closed with a twisting action, in the same way that jump rings are opened and closed (see p.112).

8 Applications of the screw

WORK IN SILVER AND OTHER METALS would scarcely be possible without the aid of those basic mechanisms we often take for granted. Levers such as pliers and hammers enhance the power of our hands and arms, and the screw can, with ingenuity, be utilised in a variety of ways. Vices, whether handheld or fixed, rely on the screw as does, in a very different way, the micrometer.

Swaging is a metalworking technique which utilises steel tools to force the metal into shape; a rifle bullet, for example, is constructed using the swaging process. This simple swaging tool consists of two steel cones threaded onto a nut and bolt. The device and variants of it can be used to make a range of projects, from rings to catches.

The nut and bolt should be of good quality, as the repeated tightening and untightening can lead to wear on the thread. The example in the picture below is made from stainless steel. The M12 bolt is 50 mm (2 in.) with a

A selection of rings (RIGHT), which can be made using the swaging tool (BELOW).

hexagonal head, and there are two washers, one under each cone. It may be better to use a finer or slower thread than this if one is available. A slow thread requiring a greater number of turns to move the nut a given distance will enable a greater force to be applied. The hexagonal head will enable the bolt to be securely held in a vice.

The cones are made from a 25 mm (1 in.) diameter mild-steel bar drilled with a 12 mm (½ in.) hole to be a snug fit on the bolt. Wheel nuts from a car can be used, but these are not as reliable as this item, which is turned on a lathe. The chamfer is 45 degrees, and the finish of this surface should be very smooth. The chamfer does not come to a sharp edge at the hole; there should be a slight flat on the end. If the inside edge of the chamfer is about 15 mm (⅝ in.), this should fit inside the smallest of rings. The outside diameter of 25 mm (1 in.) will accommodate all but the largest and narrowest of rings.

BRONZE RING WITH SILVER LINING

Bronze is a beautiful metal often neglected by the jewellery maker. An alloy of copper and tin, it has a rich, warm colour, and with age it tarnishes into a distinctive patina. Its usefulness to the craftsman is perhaps inhibited by the fact that tarnished metal will stain the wearer's skin. A happy solution to this problem is this bronze ring with its silver lining. As the bronze becomes tarnished, the silver, which can be seen at the edges and through the holes, provides a contrast with the patina of the bronze.

The process of swaging rounds off the inside of the ring nicely, making it more comfortable for the wearer. It also ensures that the bronze is not in contact with the skin. This project is a good test of soldering skills, as the join will be subjected to greater force than usual.

YOU WILL NEED:

◆ Swaging tool

◆ 0.5 mm (B&S 24) silver sheet, 12 mm (½ in.) wide, the length of the wearer's ring size (see p.140)

◆ 0.8 mm (B&S 20) bronze sheet, 12 mm (½ in.) wide, the length of the wearer's ring size plus 4 mm.

1. Punch the line of holes in the bronze strip using a 4 mm ($^1/_8$ in.) peg in the die to make sure that all are equally spaced. Establish the length of blank required, allowing an extra 4 mm ($^1/_8$ in.) of length compared to the silver lining.

2. Using the rolling mill, stretch the metal until the required length corresponds to the correct position of the holes when cut to length. There must, of course, be a large hole at one end and a small hole at the other. On the finished ring all the holes should be the same distance apart. Trim the strip to an even width of about 10 mm ($^3/_8$ in.) with shears, then bend into position for soldering.

3. Bend the silver strip into position to form the lining. After soldering, remove any surplus solder from both rings with a file and emery boards. Make both rings round using a mallet; the lining should be a snug fit in the bronze ring.

4. Finish the edges of both rings on emery boards, checking the width of each all round with dividers. It is very important that both ring and liner are equally soft. If there is the slightest chance that either has been work-hardened, they must be annealed. Both rings must be polished before they are fitted together on the swaging device.

5. Hold the bolt in the vice horizontally and thread on the cones with the rings between them. Slowly tighten the nut while holding the bronze ring in the middle of the liner. As the edges of the liner begin to swell, making the outer ring captive, remove the work from the device and check that the liner is distorting evenly all round. Any areas which are moving too much can be lightly hammered back while the work is held on a ring mandrel. Parts of the work which distort less can be tapped down with the edge of a mallet while they are held on the swaging tool. When the rings are firmly and evenly united, polish with powdered rouge and a soft cloth.

The overall length of the ring blank is 66 mm.

CHASED RING 1

The swaging system, which joins two thin rings together to make one thicker ring, makes it possible to use chasing techniques where punches are used to create deeply embossed designs on the thin metal. The lining doubles the thickness of the ring, making it as strong as if it were made from a single piece of thicker metal.

The punches used on this project are all made from oval nails, which lends a kind of unity to the final piece. A four-inch nail will make a punch of just the right length. Punches made for a particular project, such as this one, will start a collection that you can add to for subsequent projects.

A nail, which is made of mild steel, cannot be hardened like the best-quality repoussé punches, but the need for hardness in this type of punch is questionable. Both the annealed metal being worked on, and the yielding material underneath it, are very soft, so the nail is hard enough for its purpose.

Start a collection of punches to be added to with subsequent projects. From left to right: small diameter lining punch, large blocking punch, matting punch, large diameter lining punch, small blocking punch.

Blocking punches, which are used to punch-up the metal from the reverse, can be made using the head of the nail for the large size, and the shank for the smaller size. Begin by filing or grinding the end flat, and then file a bevel all round it. Using files and emery cloth, round off the end until a smooth, even shape is achieved. As these punches are used on the back of the work, polishing will not be necessary.

Lining punches, for tracing the outline of the ovals, are made by sawing off the point of the nail, and sawing or grinding a bevel on the end. A half-round needle file has been used to create the half oval shape in the punches pictured right.) Make one for the side, and one for the end of the oval.

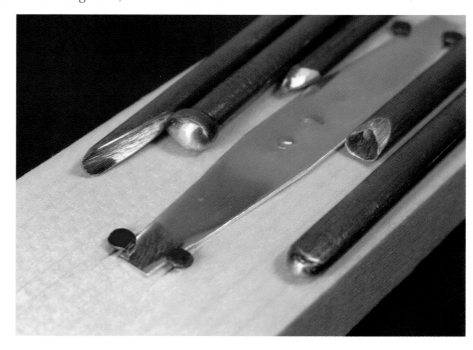

A matting punch, used to make the background pattern, is a small oval made by grinding the end of the nail to a point and filing the face until the size is just right. Matting is carried out on a hard surface, brass being the most often used. The harder surface can lead to wear on the nails, so a centre punch made of harder steel can be ground down for the purpose.

A 12 mm (½ in.) square block of hardwood, such as oak, is used as a punch instead of a mallet for flattening areas of the work where there is risk of damage to the pattern. Two working surfaces are required, a smooth steel or brass plate and a more yielding surface such as softwood or lead.

TIP   IF LEAD IS USED WITH SILVER, GREAT CARE MUST BE TAKEN TO CLEAN THE METAL BEFORE IT IS HEATED, AS TINY TRACES OF LEAD ON THE SURFACE OF THE SILVER WILL CAUSE IT TO MELT.

YOU WILL NEED:

- Swaging tool (see p.84)
- 0.5 mm (B&S 24) silver sheet, 12 mm (½ in.) wide and the length of the wearer's ring size (see p.140 for ring sizing)
- 0.5 mm (B&S 24) silver sheet, 12 mm (½ in.) wide, 4 mm longer than the wearer's ring size
- Broad-headed nails (upholsterer's tacks would be suitable)
- Block of soft wood

1. Begin by cutting the longer of the two strips to shape. This should be about 12 mm (½ in.) wide in the middle, tapering to about 6 mm (¼ in.) at either end. Fasten the blank to the wooden block with broad-headed nails.

2. Use as heavy a hammer as you can manage, preferably one with a broad head which is less likely to miss its mark. With the work face down, punch up the three ovals, then turn the work over and trace the outlines with the lining punches. Having made the first mark, move the punch around the oval, resting it in the end of the existing groove to make a continuous line. To follow the smaller curve at the end, lean the punch slightly towards the outside of the oval so that only the middle of the punch is in contact with the metal.

3. With the work resting on the steel or brass block, punch in the background with the little oval-shaped matting punch. Keep the oval in the same direction, either across or along the work, and try to keep the marks close to but not overlapping each other. It may be necessary to turn the work over and reinforce the large ovals, and to retrace the lines around them from the front. When the punching is complete, trim each side as necessary to make sure the design is in the middle of the strip.

4. Measure the length and make sure that the lining is 4 mm (⅛ in.) shorter and the same shape as the outer layer, before bending both rings into shape for soldering.

TIP   TRY NOT TO LOOK AT WHERE THE HAMMER IS STRIKING THE PUNCH. THE EYE SHOULD BE ON THE TIP OF THE PUNCH WHERE, IT MEETS THE WORK PIECE.

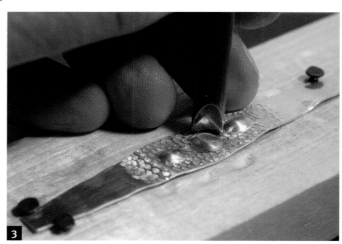
3

5. Solder both rings, clean off any surplus solder and make both round using the ring mandrel.

6. Ensure that one ring is a good fit inside the other, and thread both onto the swaging device. Tighten the nut to make the outer ring captive as in the bronze ring with silver lining project (see p.85). The difference in width between the rings from front to back makes no difference to the swaging process. The rings are simply pushed to one side on the bolt.

CHASED RING 2

This project requires three more punches, all made from nails. The first is made from a six-inch nail cut down to 100 mm (4 in.) long. File the end flat and square, and drill with a centre drill to create a little circle. The sharp edge must be rounded off slightly to avoid cutting the metal. The second punch is a four-inch round nail, rounded off at the end to a domed shape. A little dot punch made from a four-inch nail or from a centre punch completes the set (see picture below).

TIP HARDWOOD PUNCHES, BOTH ROUNDED AND CHISEL-EDGED, CAN BE USED WITH GREATER ACCURACY THAN A MALLET.

YOU WILL NEED:

- Swaging tool (see p.84)
- 0.5 mm (B&S 24) silver sheet for the lining ring, 12 mm (½ in.) wide and the length of the wearer's ring size (see p.140)
- 0.5 mm (B&S 24) silver sheet for the outer ring, 12 mm (½ in.) wide and 4 mm longer than the length of the lining

1. Using a permanent pen divide the blank for the outer ring along its length into equal sections, and mark the centre of each section. Alternatively, use a piece of wire mesh as a guide for the punch. This one (see picture right) is from an old bird feeder and, used diagonally, makes circles about 8 mm apart. Punch the row of circles, then turn the work over and raise the little domes from the reverse, using the 4-four-inch rounded nail. Repeat this process until a distinct line of domes has been made.

2. Punch in the background with the little dot punch. The size of each tiny circle will significantly affect the appearance of the background, so try out different-sized punches on scrap metal before working on the finished project. When bending into shape for soldering, take care that the background does not bend too sharply; the domes will not bend at all.

3. Make the lining ring and swage it into place (see p.86).

TIP   FROM TIME TO TIME, AS THE WORK BECOMES DISTORTED, IT WILL BE NECESSARY TO TURN THE BLANK OVER AND FLATTEN IT OUT WITH A MALLET OR HARDWOOD PUNCH.

TIP   CHASED WORK OF THIS KIND IS USUALLY OXIDISED AND THEN POLISHED TO ACCENTUATE THE DIFFERENCE BETWEEN THE BACKGROUND AND THE HIGH SPOTS. LIVER OF SULPHUR IS USED FOR THIS PROCESS (SEE P.50).

RING WITH A GYPSY SETTING

A true gypsy setting involves some very tricky fitting and filing, making it beyond the scope of this book and all but the most experienced of jewellery makers. This alternative or faux gypsy setting makes use of the swaging tool and a punch and die.

YOU WILL NEED:

♦ Swaging tool (see p.84)

♦ 6 mm (¼ in.) diameter cabochon

♦ 0.5 mm (B&S 24) silver sheet for the lining ring, 12 mm (½ in.) wide and the length of the wearer's ring size (see p.140)

♦ 0.5 mm (B&S 24) silver sheet for the outer ring, 12 mm (½ in.) wide and 5 mm longer than the length of the lining

Note: The width of the metal at its widest point, which is alongside the setting, is determined by the size of the cabochon. There must be a minimum of 3 mm (⅛ in.) either side of a 6 mm (¼ in.) stone, making this example 12 mm (½ in.) wide, tapering to 6 mm (¼ in.) at either end. For larger sizes of stone there must be even more room either side. The difference in length between the outer ring and the lining ring must be 5 mm (³/₁₆ in.), to allow for the insertion of the cabochon. The hole must be 0.5 mm smaller than the cabochon, in this example 5.5 mm.

1. After punching the hole for the cabochon and soldering both rings, make them round on a ring mandrel and polish them.

2. Using pliers, make a small flat area on the inner ring at the point where the setting will be when the rings are threaded together. Insert the inner ring, leaving a gap just big enough to push in the cabochon.

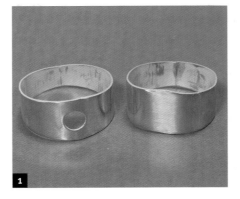

3. With the cabochon in place, squeeze the rings together and force them together on the swaging tool as before (see p.86).

4. The cabochon is now securely fixed, but you will find there is a void around the setting which needs to be closed up. Thread the ring onto a ring mandrel, and force it down the mandrel with a mallet. If necessary, the area around the cab may be pushed down with a wooden punch, taking care not to mark the surface of the metal.

5. Finish the edges on emery boards and polish with powdered rouge.

KINETIC JEWELLERY: THE FIDDLING RING

It has been said that if you give a a ring to someone you care for, the design of which encourages the wearer to play with it, every time they do so they will think of you. These movable rings are sometimes called kinetic jewellery. The swaging tool is ideally suited to the creation of these multi-part rings.

The inner ring in this kind of project must be made of slightly thicker metal than that used to line rings which are tightly fixed together. The soldered joint must be especially secure, as unlike a lining with another ring around it, this ring is unsupported during the swaging process.

The amount of clearance between the inner and outer rings is important. The outer ring or rings must be allowed to move freely, but there must be no risk of them coming off the inner ring altogether. The swaging cannot be too pronounced or the ring becomes uncomfortable. When three or more rings are captive, the middle one can have greater clearance, as to become free it must pass over the outer rings.

Rings of different materials and sections provide variety, and there is almost no limit to the number of rings that can be used. The left hand ring shown at the bottom of the previous page is made from alternate silver, gold and bronze rings, amounting to five rings in all. Rings can be stacked on top of each other as well as side by side.

TIP   SINCE IT DOES NOT RELY ON HEAT FOR JOINING, THE SWAGING SYSTEM CAN BE USED TO COMBINE NON-METALS WITH SILVER. RINGS MADE FROM PORCELAIN, GLASS OR SEMI-PRECIOUS STONES, WHICH BY THEMSELVES MAY BE TOO BRITTLE TO BE WORN AS JEWELLERY, WILL BE GIVEN SOME PROTECTION BY THE ADDITION OF A LINER. THE CONTROL PROVIDED BY THE SCREW THREAD MEANS THAT THESE FRAGILE PARTS CAN BE JOINED TOGETHER WITH GREAT DELICACY.

PENANNULAR THUMB RING

YOU WILL NEED:

- Swaging tool (see p.84)
- Strip of adhesive paper
- 0.5 mm (B&S 24) silver sheet for the inner ring, 15 mm (⁵/₈ in.) wide, fitted to the length of the wearer's thumb.
- 0.5 mm (B&S 24) silver sheet for the outer ring, 15 mm (⁵/₈ in.) wide, 0.5 mm longer than the inner ring

A ring to be worn on the thumb must take account of the fact that the knuckle over which it must pass is considerably wider than the part of the thumb on which it will eventually rest. The ring which passes over the knuckle will almost certainly be too loose when in place. One solution is to make a ring which opens and closes or, as in this example, two open rings,

The penannular thumb ring can be opened and closed.

one sliding within the other. With the rings rubbing against one another, and likely to scratch each other, the metal used has been rolled with a pattern to minimise the effect of any scratches.

1. Measure the thumb using a strip of adhesive paper, and cut the two rings to length. To give greater stiffness to the ring, this example has been made 15 mm wide; the outer ring is 5 mm longer than the inner one.

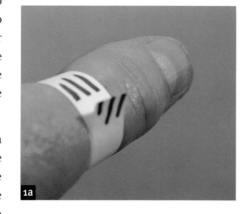

2. After soldering, give both rings a preliminary polish to help to ensure that they slide easily together. Place the ring in the swaging tool with the joins alongside each other and force them together as before (see p.86).

3. Hold the joined rings in a vice and, with a piercing saw, cut out the section of the ring that includes the join to about a quarter of its circumference. The gap created will almost certainly be too small, but it is just as important that it is not too large. Cut off a small amount at a time, trying the ring on as you go, until the gap is just wide enough to slide over the thumb. Round off the edges of both rings with emery boards and a polishing machine until they slide together smoothly but not too freely.

TIP　FOR A LITTLE EXTRA INTEREST MORE RINGS CAN BE ADDED BEFORE THE SWAGING PROCESS. THESE MUST BE FAIRLY SOLID AND PLANISHED ON THE SIDES TO MAKE THEM LESS LIKELY TO OPEN OUT. THESE ADDITIONAL RINGS MAY MAKE THE OVERALL RING A LITTLE MORE SECURE, BUT THEIR MAIN FUNCTION IS TO PROVIDE SOMETHING EXTRA TO FIDDLE WITH.

9 The removable spindle tool

THERE ARE TWO SITUATIONS WHERE IT CAN BE ADVISABLE to make a forming tool: when it is difficult to achieve the desired result with conventional tools, or when the tool to be made will have many applications in the making of future projects. The removable spindle tool appears to satisfy both criteria.

One of the challenges facing the jewellery maker is the creation of identical sets of components or units. The scroll link is one such component. The removable spindle tool is the only practical way that this unit can be made, and will allow the making of lots of similar units.

The device is designed to hold thin strips of metal securely, leaving both hands free to form the metal with great precision. Being largely made of wood, the device leaves no tool marks on the work. There is a limit to the thickness of the metal that can be formed on the device, and as with all forming processes it will always be necessary to anneal the metal being formed.

The tool consists of a piece of plywood with a triangular piece cut out from the top edge, and a series of holes along its side. Bolted to this is a lever made up of two strips of plywood joined to each other, with another piece of plywood between them. The length of the lever should be long enough to pass over the square base section.

1. Begin by drilling a 6 mm (¼ in.) hole in the corner of the square base, 12 mm (½ in.) in from both edges. Cut out the V-shape shown in the diagram opposite, along the top edge and round off the corners.

2. Cut out the two sides of the lever and the spacing piece. Drill the 3 mm (⅛ in.) and 6 mm (¼ in.) holes with both halves pinned together, to

YOU WILL NEED:

- Plywood, 150 x 125 x 12 mm (6 x 5 x ½ in.)
- Two plywood strips, 200 x 65 x 12 mm (8 x 2½ x ½ in.)
- Plywood, 40 x 40 x 12 mm (1¾ x 1¾ x ½ in.)
- Glue and small wood screws
- 3-inch nail
- 50 mm bolt M6 with nut and washers

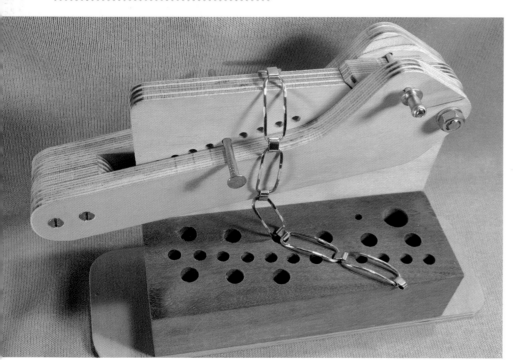

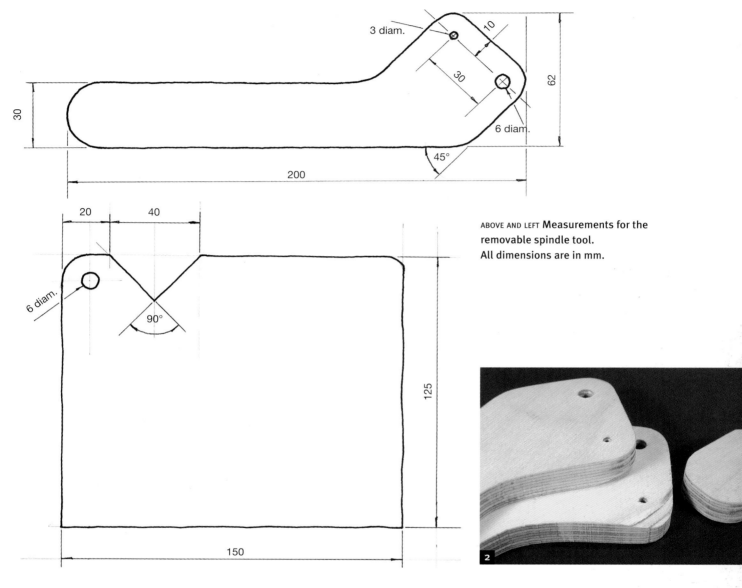

3 diam.

10

30

6 diam.

62

30

45°

200

20   40

6 diam.

90°

125

150

ABOVE AND LEFT **Measurements for the removable spindle tool. All dimensions are in mm.**

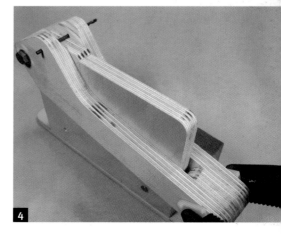

make sure the holes are perfectly aligned. At this stage, before the sides are glued together, make the chamfer above the 3 mm ($^1/_8$ in.) holes on the inside of each side using a rasp and glass paper.

3. Make the triangular anvil by sawing the 40 mm (1¾ in.) square of plywood diagonally in half. Round off the corners and rub down both sides using glass paper to make them slightly thinner than the base. This will prevent the anvil sticking in between the arms of the lever.

4. Bolt the two sides either side of the base and insert a 2.5 mm drill bit through the 3 mm ($^1/_8$ in.) holes. With this spindle resting on the plywood anvil, the two halves of the lever will be in the correct position to be glued

together. When the glue has dried, drill two holes on either side and insert screws to secure the joint. Finally, the end can be smoothed with glass paper.

5. With the device assembled and the spindle in place on the anvil, mark the position of the first and last hole in the line of holes in the base. The first hole is marked with a 2 mm spacer under the spindle, and then with the spacer removed the position of the last hole can be located. The remaining holes can now be drilled on a straight line between these two points. These are 4 mm ($^1/_8$ in) in diameter and should be about 10 mm ($^3/_8$ in.) apart.

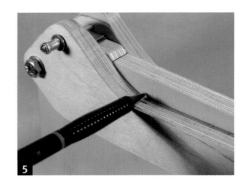

6. Whatever the thickness of the work being held, the lever can now be locked in position with a three-inch nail. The point of the nail should be ground down, rounded and polished, so that it slides easily into the holes.

The removable spindle device can be held in a vice or bolted to a block of wood. The block itself can be screwed to a plywood base, allowing the whole assembly to be clamped to the table. The hardwood block in this example is drilled with a series of holes to accommodate a range of steel pegs and stakes. A small strip of wood or plastic sharpened to a wedge will be required to start the rolling-up process. The chamfer on the inside edges of the lever allows fingers to get closer to the metal being formed.

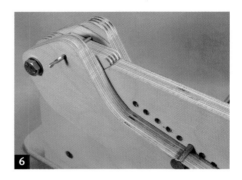

The width of metal that can be formed on the device is limited by the 12 mm ($^1/_2$ in.) thickness of the plywood. If this were to be increased, there is a greater risk of the spindle bending under pressure, which of course would make the device ineffective.

THE SCROLL LINK

The scroll link can be made from silver as thin as 0.3 mm (B&S 29); this one is 4.5 mm wide. Such thin metal can be used because the way the scroll link is made, with some parts of double thickness, adds to the strength of the thin metal. As a link in a chain it is far superior to and just as strong as a wire jump ring. The little scroll, or variations of it, may also be preferred to a jump ring as a hanging device for a pendant.

> **YOU WILL NEED:**
> ◆ Thin silver sheet, 4.5 x 30 mm

The disadvantage of the scroll link is that it cannot be opened and closed like a jump ring, and therefore the links it joins must be soldered around it. The scroll link must always be the first part of the chain or pendant to be made, and is usually complete and polished before beginning work on the rest of the project.

1. Begin by cutting out the thin strips. Use dividers set to 4.5 mm to scribe a line parallel to the edge of the sheet. A sheared cut will always leave one edge neater than the other, so after each cut is made with shears, turn the sheet over to scribe the next line on the underside. By this means, both

edges of each strip will have neat rounded edges on the top surface, and a less attractive edge underneath. Cut the strips to 30 mm (1⅛ in.) long.

2. Place the end of the strip, with its good side facing down, under the spindle – in this case a 2.5 mm drill bit, and clamp it in place with the nail (see picture 4a, opposite). Before exerting pressure, make sure that both the work and the spindle are properly positioned. The device is capable of applying considerable force, which could cause damage to both the work and to the device itself if it is not used with care.

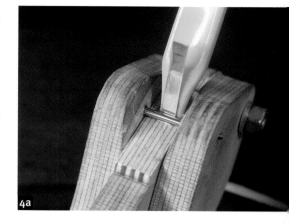
4a

3. Push the little plastic lever under the metal and bend it upwards to wrap it closely around the drill. Once the bend is started you can use your fingers to press the thin metal tightly around the drill bit. Release the lever and pull the strip around until it stands up square to the anvil, then lock it again with the nail. Check that the very end of the strip is properly wrapped around the spindle and, if necessary, tap it down with a flat punch before pressing down the long end with a finger.

4b

4. With the first coil made, measure the remaining straight section of metal. Bend it a little at a time, measuring after each slight bend until the straight section is 15 mm (⅝ in.) long, half the length of the strip. Remove the spindle and the half-completed scroll will fall free. It is important not to bend the metal too far, as bending it backwards will leave a kink in it that will show up clearly on the polished face. Repeat the process on the other end of the strip until the two scrolls meet.

5. To make them strong enough the scrolls must be soldered together. This is a fairly straightforward soldering job, as the solder will usually flow naturally between the coils. Use narrow pallions of easy solder placed along the join. Do not overheat this kind of structure as the thin silver is easily melted.

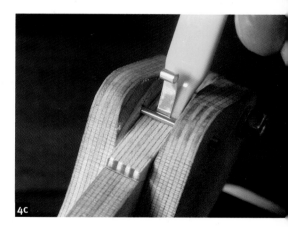
4c

6. With the scroll joined at the centre, the holes can be forced open slightly with a broaching tool. This is just a smooth round tapered rod, which can be made from a steel knitting needle, preferably mounted in a wooden handle. Pushed into each side of the holes using a twisting motion, it will force the inside layer against the outside, and will make the holes properly round. This process will also harden the metal slightly. Rub both sides of each unit on an emery board to make them smooth, and to eliminate any inaccuracies.

7. The polishing of these units is made more difficult because of their small size. This little holding device (opposite) is a brass rod bent in two until it fits the holes in the scroll. Held in this way all the units can be polished as one, with little risk of their being dropped.

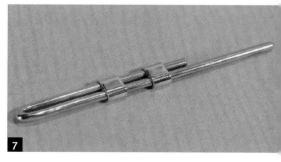
7

8. Clean out the insides of the holes using polishing string. Thread the scrolls on one side of the brass rod to keep them together, and thread the string into the row of holes on each side in turn. A long bootlace fixed to the bench serves the purpose, and the ferrule on the end makes it easier to thread it into the hole.

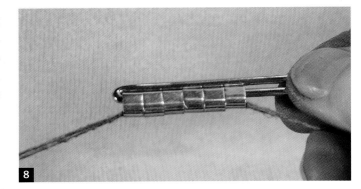

9. When the scroll link is the last link in a chain, and therefore one half of the fastening device, it will need to be tapered slightly to fit the bolt ring. Make a holding device of two sawn-off nails driven into the end of a small block of wood spaced to fit the holes in the scroll. This will be enough to hold the work securely and make the filing process easier.

SCROLL-LINK BRACELET

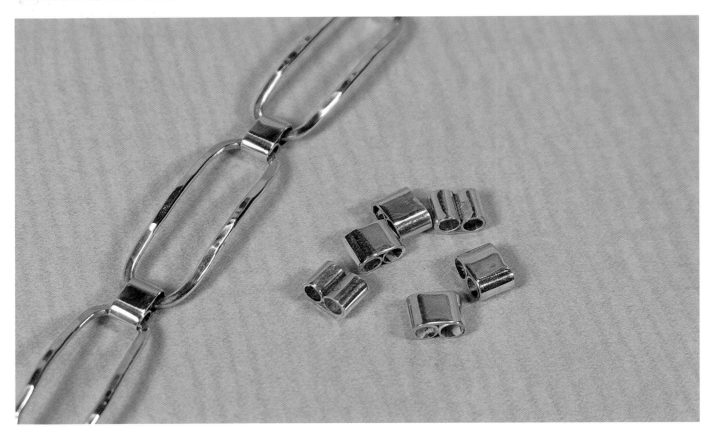

This bracelet consists of five links and five scrolls. Each link is made from a piece of 1.5 mm (B&S 15) round silver wire 70 mm (2¾ in.) long. The overall length of the bracelet is about 190 mm (7½ in.). The scrolls are made from 0.3 mm (B&S 29) thick silver, 30 mm (1¼ in.) long by 4.5 mm wide.

YOU WILL NEED:

♦ 1.5 mm (B&S 15) round silver wire

♦ 0.3 mm (B&S 29) silver sheet

♦ Fastening for the chain

To determine the lengths of silver wire and sheet required, see left.

To establish the exact finished length of a bracelet you can wrap a length of string or wire around the wrist and measure it. A dressmaker's tape measure can also be used, but nothing serves the purpose as well as a chain. A length of brass chain from an ironmonger's shop with a hook at one end makes the ideal template. The chain is wrapped around the wrist and the hook fastened to one of the links. Worn in this way, the chain will give an accurate impression of how the bracelet will feel in use.

A length of chain is the best way to measure the length required for a bracelet

Having established the length of bracelet required, you need to decide on the number and length of the links. The links in this sample bracelet are made from different lengths of wire. The longest link is made using a 70 mm (2¾ in.) length of wire, with each link reduced by 5 mm, down to 40 mm (1½ in.) for the shortest link. By using these two chains, it is possible to plan the project, and so avoid the costly mistake of a bracelet that is either too long or too short. The type of fastening must also be considered, as this will affect length, and some fastenings need more slack in the chain than others.

1. Make the scroll links first (see p.96) and finish them completely, including the polishing stage. Make the long links up to the soldering stage, being particularly careful to make well-fitting joints, as these links will be subjected to considerable force later in the process. When bending the wire try to avoid making sharp corners, around which the scroll links may not pass.

A length of chain can be used as a template.

2. Join up the chain, making sure that all the scroll links face the same way. At this stage a fastening device must be decided on; it may have to be threaded onto the last link before soldering. Flux the joins and lay out the work on the soldering block with the joins furthest away from the heat. Make the joins using a generous amount of easy solder. After pickling and rinsing thoroughly, tap each link roughly into shape with a mallet.

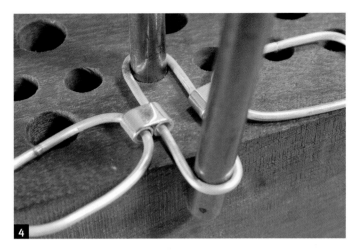

3. The next stage involves drilling a row of holes in a block of hardwood. The holes are 6.4 mm in diameter, and the block can be the same one that supports the removable spindle tool. The line of holes, which are about 12 mm (½ in.) apart, is at an angle to the front edge of the block. Two six-inch nails, one of which is sawn in half, and both of which are smooth and polished, complete this device.

4. Each link can now be straightened by placing it over the sawn-off nail in one of the holes and levering with the other nail, the end of which is positioned against the front edge of the block. Do this more than once, moving the nail along the row to a hole further away from the edge. This process makes each end of the link perfectly round.

5. The leverage generates considerable force and will clearly test the soldered joint. For the link to be made completely straight, the wire must be slightly stretched. It will be obvious that the delicate scroll links need to be positioned well clear of either nail, and not trapped under the link being straightened, before any force is applied.

6. Bend each link around a cylindrical stake – scaffold pipe was used to make this example – and lightly planish each half of each link in turn. The edges can also be planished by inserting a strip of hardwood of the correct thickness into the link and resting it on a flat stake. At each stage be careful not to catch the delicate scroll links with the hammer; if damaged they will be almost impossible to repair.

7. Polish each link separately, holding the rest of the chain in the palm of the hand, out of the way of the polishing mop. As with all chains, final polishing can be done using powdered rouge on a soft cloth, with one end of the chain fixed to the bench and the other held in the hand.

SCROLL-LINK BRACELET WITH BEADS

YOU WILL NEED:

◆ 1.5 mm (B&S 15) silver wire, cut into 90 mm (3½ in.) lengths for each link required

◆ 16 8 mm (⁵/₁₆ in.) beads

◆ 0.6 mm (B&S 23) silver wire, 300 mm (12 in.) long

◆ 0.3 (B&S 30) silver sheet, cut into four 30 x 5 mm (1¹/₈ x ¼ in.) strips

◆ 12 mm (½ in.) bolt ring

The forming of these bracelet links need not be restricted to the use of six-inch nails. In this version 8 mm (⁵/₁₆ in.) rods are used, the wider link allowing for a slightly wider scroll link. The slightly greater width in the scroll makes for a stronger link and also improves the appearance of the bracelet. It also makes it possible to thread 8 mm (⁵/₁₆ in.) beads into the links. These lie next to the skin, making this a very comfortable bracelet to wear.

1. This example has four sections, each made from 90 mm (3½ in.) of 1.5 mm (B&S 15) wire. The beads are threaded onto 0.6 mm (B&S 23) wire, and the threading must follow a particular pattern. After assembling and careful soldering, form the links as before, and planish each link until the wire is slightly flattened.

2. Cut the thin wire to 300 mm (12 in.) long and wrap the end around the frame four times, pulling each coil tight as you do so. The slightly flattened cross section of the wire makes it possible to pull the thin wire around the frame without it uncoiling from the other end. Leave a short length of wire to be trimmed to size later.

3. Thread on the first bead; to ensure that it lies in the centre of the sides of the frame, the thin wire must pass from the bottom of one side of the frame to the top of the other side of the frame, or from top to bottom. Wrap the wire four times around the opposite side and thread on the second bead.

The thin wire wound around the frame must always pass from top of the frame to the bottom or the bottom to the top.

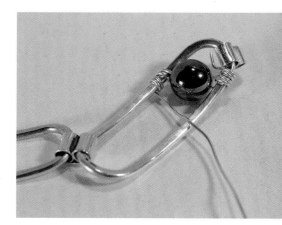

4. When the first three beads are in place the short length of wire can be trimmed off. Cut off the surplus with side cutters so that just enough remains to be pushed against the inside of the frame with a bezel pusher or a burnisher. In this way the sharp end of wire will be out of the way and will not scratch the skin or snag on clothing.

5. Thread the final bead and trim the end of the wire as described in step 4. Each little group of four coiled wires can now be squeezed together with pliers, and the beads pushed up or down the frame so that an equal space is left at either end.

Pushing down the loose end of wire with a burnisher.

PENDANT WITH BEADS

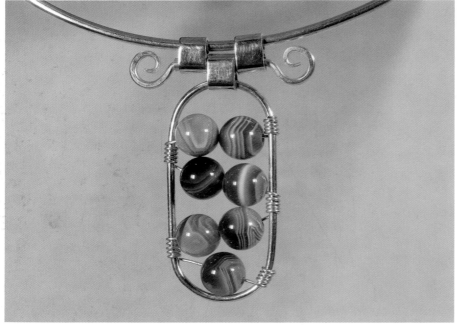

A pendant to match the bracelet can be made the same size as one of the four units of the bracelet, or made wider to allow for a different arrangement of beads. The scroll link makes an ideal bail. The bail on a pendant can be an important element in the design, and can often make a plain and simple project into something special.

The wider cartouche shape is formed using two 16 mm (⁵⁄₈ in.) steel rods and a hole in a block of wood (see right). Always remember to keep the bail well clear of the former when applying force in this way.

The wider pendant, as well as using more beads, also allows for a wider and more complex hanging system. Three scrolls with a wire scroll between them make for a more elaborate effect. In this example (above) a short length of chenier is inserted within the three scrolls to keep them aligned.

Using steel rods as a former generates a lot of force with its attendant risks.

length of chenier is inserted within the three scrolls to keep them aligned. A single bail made from a tapered strip of silver shows off the double thickness of the metal, adding extra interest.

Cut out a triangle 10 mm (³/₈ in.) at the base and about 35 mm (1³/₈ in.) long, from 0.3 mm (B&S 29) silver sheet. Cut off the corners to about 8 mm (⁵/₁₆ in.) to make the last section parallel, or slightly tapered, towards the base. This will ensure that no sharp corners protrude at the widest part of the finished scroll. The narrow end of the unit must be wound a little more to make an extra layer of metal at the narrow end, to compensate for the lack of width.

This tapered version of the scroll can be used at the end of a bracelet to make one half of the catch, when the other half is a bolt ring. When used for this purpose it may be necessary to file each side to a smooth and even taper. Use the holding device on p.98 for this operation.

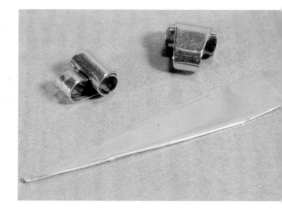

ABOVE **Two finished bails, and the tapered silver strip required to make them.**

BELOW **The bail in use.**

PENANNULAR BROOCH

The penannular brooch can be used to pin a shawl or a scarf, or as a decorative item in itself. There are many examples of this type of jewellery in the Celtic tradition, many of them very ornate and set with precious stones. The word 'penannular' means a broken or part ring, and the brooch works by the pin being lined up with the gap in the ring and threaded into the cloth; the ring is then twisted around under the pin to lock the pin into place.

These plain examples of the brooch rely on the rolled-up eye at the end of the pin and on the forged and planished ends to the rings for their effectiveness.

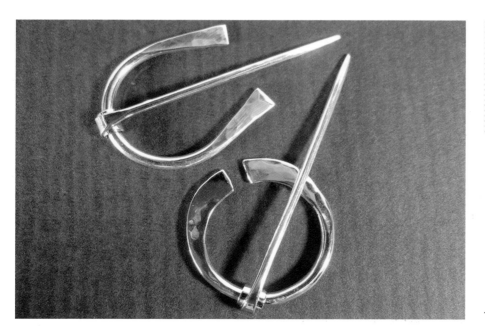

The penannular brooch.

> **YOU WILL NEED:**
>
> ◆ 1.8 mm (B&S 13) silver wire, 70 mm (2¾ in.) long
>
> ◆ 2.5 mm (B&S 10) silver wire, 75 mm (3 in.) long.

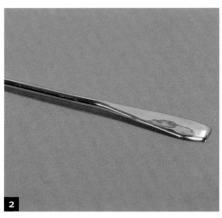

TIP   THE USE OF A SLIGHTLY
ROUNDED HAMMER AND STAKE WILL
HELP TO SPREAD THE METAL AND
INCREASE ITS WIDTH.

1. Make the pin first. Forge the end of a piece of 1.8 mm (B&S 13) wire with a rounded hammer on a rounded stake to make a flattened end. The flat section must be about 0.3 mm thick for about 12 mm (½ in.) of its length, tapering gradually for a further 8 mm ($^5/_{16}$ in.).

2. Finish the forging on a flat stake and then anneal the flattened section of the pin. As this thin area will heat up more quickly than the round part, concentrate the heat on the round section to make sure that all of the metal to be forged is softened.

3. Roll up the end around a 2.5 mm drill bit, cut it to a length of about 60 mm ($2^3/_8$ in.) and file a long taper on the end. Finish the pin by planishing, rolling the pin across a flat stake as the hammer strikes the whole surface of the metal. This process will harden and straighten the pin and will also impart a polish to the metal.

4. The broken ring is made from 2.5 mm (B&S 10) silver wire, 75 mm (3 in.) long. The horseshoe shape is the easiest to form, as it only requires bending the wire with fingers around a 25 mm (1 in.) bar; the two ends will always remain straight. Forge the ends by making a fishtail at each end and then working back along the bar to make a gradual taper. Remember to thread on the pin before forging the second taper. Trim the ends with shears before polishing both parts to remove any sharp corners and edges.

5. To make the round version of the brooch, the rounded ring must be soldered closed before it is forged flat. As the pin must be attached before the join is made, and making the ring round with the pin in place would be difficult, the ring must be made round before it is soldered. Wrap the 2.5 mm (B&S 10) wire around a wooden dowel of 25 mm (1 in.) diameter and saw through where the two ends overlap. Next thread on the completed pin, then solder the ends together. With the joint closed, the area around the join can now be forged flat.

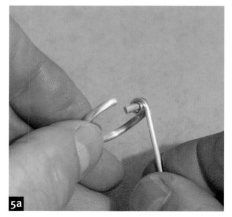

TIP IT MAY BE NECESSARY TO OPEN OUT THE EYE SLIGHTLY WITH A TAPERED PIN TO MAKE IT FIT THE RING.

6. Some distortion of the circle is to be expected at this stage. To restore the roundness of the ring, use a round bar with an 8 mm ($^5/_{16}$ in.) blind hole drilled in its side; in this example a hammer has been used (see picture 6). This hole will make room for the rolled-up end of the pin. Hold the steel bar firmly, close to the vice with the hole on its side. The steel rod or hammer is, of course, smaller than the inside diameter of the ring, but by twisting it to a slight angle, a fit will be made to create a workable stake.

7. When the forging is finished, the join can be opened again to create the essential gap. This gap should be as narrow as possible, being just wide enough for the pin to pass through it.

PENDANT BAILS

It is sometimes useful to roll up a hanging device on the pendant itself, making a separate bail unnecessary. Although there are limits to the width and thickness of metal which can be formed in this way, the removable spindle tool can be used. In the narrow drop shape shown below there is no room for a hole to be drilled so the rolled-up bail is the only option. Making the rolled-up section thin enough can be achieved with a hammer, but the rolling mill, if one is available, will make light work of this process.

When the pendant shape is too wide to fit into the spindle tool, a separate bail can be made and sweated onto the edge of the sheet. This makes for a more secure join than a simple piece of tubing would provide, and is far superior to a jump ring in a hole.

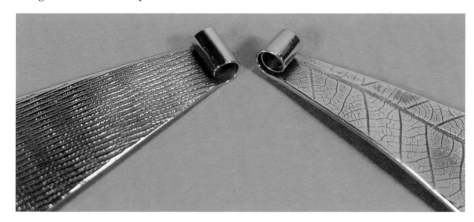

The rolled-up bail.

SOME MORE COMPLEX BAILS AND OTHER USES FOR THE REMOVABLE SPINDLE TOOL

THREE-RINGED PENDANT

YOU WILL NEED:

♦ 0.3 mm (B&S 29) silver sheet 30 x 9 mm

♦ 1.5 mm (B&S 15) round wire, cut into three lengths, 60, 90 and 120 mm (2³⁄₈, 3½ and 4¾ in.) long

♦ 0.3 mm (B&S 29) silver sheet, 38 x 8 mm

The ease with which fairly accurate units can be created using the removable spindle tool makes possible the construction of quite complex combinations. This pendant, with its three more or less concentric rings, is enhanced by the four-way bail from which the rings hang.

1. Make the first scroll from a strip of silver 30 x 9 mm using a spindle of 2.5 mm. Solder the two coils and then turn the unit over and melt two pallions of solder onto the front. Make the other half from a 38 x 8 mm silver strip. Using the same spindle, roll up the two ends until the ends are equal and the gap in the middle fits the first scroll. Melt two pallions of solder onto this part in readiness for sweating the two together.

2. Lay out the work with a pallion of solder on the two separate scrolls and the rest of the work fluxed; the two melting pallions will provide an indication of the melting of the sweated join. Finish the unit in the usual way, and polish ready for assembling the three rings.

3. The rings are made from 1.5 mm round wire, 60, 90 and 120 mm (2³⁄₈, 3½ and 4¾ in.) long. Square off the ends, thread each length of wire through the appropriate hole (as shown in the picture of the finished pendant above), and prepare for soldering. Arrange the bail and the two other rings on the side furthest from the join.

When soldering work of this kind, particularly the larger rings, two torches are invaluable. The heat can be directed to both sides of the ring and moved around to the join at the same time. In this way the solder will melt and the join will be made, without the need to heat the point furthest from the join. The bail and any other parts will not be heated and therefore will not be at risk of oxidising or annealing.

4. Make the rings round using a mallet, and planish the surface on a flat stake. Whether the surface of the work is more or less flat, or has some irregularities in it, is a matter of personal taste. When polished, this kind of beaten silver will always reflect the light well and show itself to good effect.

A simpler variation of this pendant has just two rings hanging from a bail, one side of which is made with a larger spindle. A spindle larger than the hole in the removable spindle tool can be made by threading a small piece of tubing onto the spindle. An alternative four-way bail can be created from two tapered bails soldered together.

A spindle larger than the hole in the removable spindle tool can be made by threading a small piece of tubing onto the spindle.

TUBING

From time to time it is useful to be able to make small pieces of tubing or chenier. Longer pieces are made using a drawplate, but this can be a time-consuming process and also wasteful, as more must be made than is needed. With a slight modification the removable spindle tool can be used for this purpose.

Cut a square piece of plywood a little larger than the original anvil, and draw a line from corner to corner. Mark the point on that line where the spindle will make contact with it, using the existing anvil as a template. Turn the work over and make a second mark on the opposite triangle.

Drill two holes of 3 mm (¹/₈ in.) and 3.5 mm and saw down the line to make two triangles with two half-round holes in each. With some adjustment by sanding down either side of the triangles, it will be possible to make a perfect fit between spindle and half-round hole. Make several of these triangles, each with different-sized holes. Alternatively, use a round needle file to file down the spindle's point of contact on the wooden triangle. Do this repeatedly as the spindle is reapplied to the groove.

It will now be possible to make use of the smallest offcuts of silver to make accurate tubes, U-shapes and small bails. This system can also be used to make wire scrolls, starting each one of a series in exactly the same way for an exact match. The U-tube makes a neat, concealed hanging device and can be filed flat for a good fit while being firmly held by the spindle.

These little U-shaped units can be made in various widths and from thicker metal than can be formed on the plain anvil. The half-round hole can be lined with metal by the use of tubing inserted in the larger hole, before the triangle is sawn in half in the usual way.

Making a U-shape with the spindle fitting into a half-round slot.

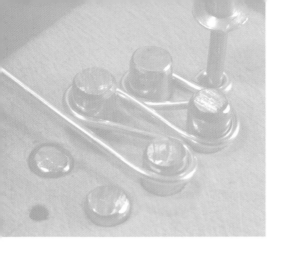

10 Findings

THIS SECTION IS LARGELY CONCERNED WITH making links, chains, catches, ear wires and the like, collectively called findings. This area of jewellery-making presents many opportunities for innovation, and for the creation of jigs, tools and other devices – useful aids in the creation of these necessary items.

Jewellery-makers often neglect to make findings, sometimes with justification. Commercially made findings are inexpensive and readily available, and there is clearly little to be gained from making items such as the rarely seen scroll at the back of an ear stud.

Nevertheless, for the amateur jewellery maker there are certain advantages to making findings. In the first place, there is the simple satisfaction of making every part of a project yourself. There is also the opportunity to create just the right link or catch, something entirely appropriate to that

A selection of commercially made findings.

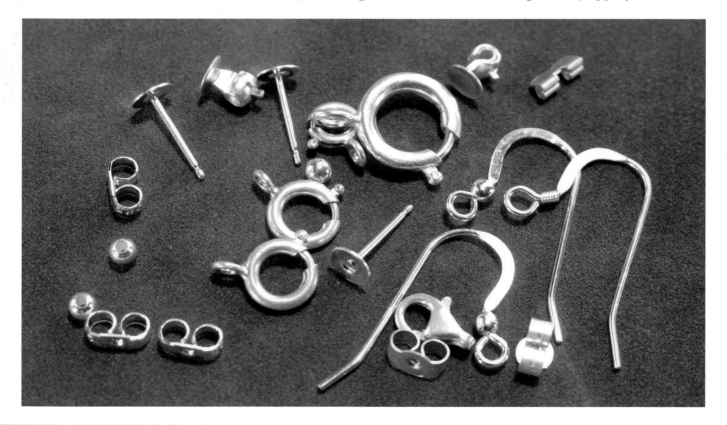

particular project. A well-designed closure will enhance any necklace or bracelet and add individuality to a piece, setting it apart from the factory-made product. A fastening need not always be hidden out of sight, but can be a prominent part of the design. The wearer of a piece of handmade jewellery will undoubtedly appreciate a distinctive catch or link, and will value the item all the more for the fact of its being unique.

MAKING JUMP RINGS

Whenever one component is connected to another in a loose, semi-permanent way – for example, a catch to a length of chain – a jump ring is used. This is a small ring, generally less than 6 mm (¼ in.) in diameter, usually made of round wire. The making of jump rings is thought by many not to be worth the effort, but there are certain advantages to making your own.

Many projects are let down by ill-considered or poorly made jump rings. Homemade jump rings are often cheaper; moreover, they can be made to a precise diameter and from exactly the right thickness of wire. The homemade jump ring does not have to be made from round wire; it may be more appropriate to make one from square or, perhaps, triangular wire. Sometimes two or more jump rings used together can enhance a project.

Jump rings are made in batches by winding a length of wire around a rod, then sawing down the coil to separate the rings. The difficulty, as with so many processes, lies in holding the work. The coil must be held firmly enough to allow the delicate blade to cut down the whole length without jamming. The blade can be trapped by the coil unwinding slightly, or it can be pinched as it approaches the bottom of the cut. Many solutions to these problems have been tried, from wrapping adhesive tape around the coil to threading the blade inside the coil and sawing outwards. None have been as effective and as easy to use as this simple device.

1. Bend the woodscrew by holding the screw section in a vice and hammering the head to an angle of about 30 degrees. Drill a hole the depth of the woodscrew about 20 mm (¾ in.) from the right-hand end and about 5 mm from the front edge.

YOU WILL NEED:

 ◆ Hardwood or plywood block,
   25 x 25 x 80 mm (1 x 1 x 3 in.)
 ◆ Woodscrew (preferably of brass)
 ◆ Panel pin

Jigs for making jump rings. A large collection of jigs will cover all eventualities.

2. Knock in the panel pin about 2 to 3 mm to the right of this hole. The head of the pin should protrude about 2 mm from the surface of the wood.

3. Screw in the woodscrew until only the smooth section protrudes and the bend points away from the front edge of the block. You will probably find it easier to use pliers against the head of the screw to do this job, rather than a screwdriver. Alternatively, grip the head of the screw in a vice and twist the block of wood.

4. Finally, saw off the head of the screw with a piercing saw and remove any sharp corners and burrs with a smooth file.

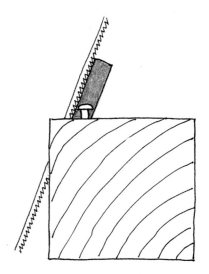

To make jump rings, hold the jig firmly in a vice, leaving plenty of room for the saw to clear the vice. Engage the end of your wire against the panel pin and wind it tightly around the screw. Six to eight rings is the optimum number to make in one batch, depending on the thickness of the wire. Use a fine blade in the piercing saw as this will be less likely to snag. Align the saw blade with the screw and saw into the wood, keeping the saw at the same angle as the screw until the saw reaches the bottom of its cut. Try to ensure that all the rings become free at the same time.

The key to making jump rings is to calculate the exact diameter of ring required, and to make it from wire of just the right thickness. This is not always easy to judge and is usually found by trial and error. The rejected rings form a collection, from among which a suitable ring may be found for a later project. Aim to make the ring as small and as unobtrusive as possible while still allowing the joined components to move freely one against the other.

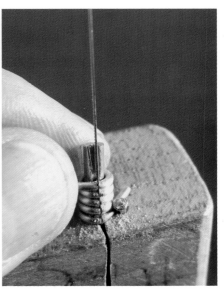

LEFT Using a piercing saw with a fine blade, try to ensure that all the rings become free at the same time.

FAR LEFT Any size of ring can be made in this way – this jig makes a ring of 13.8 mm..

CHAINS

FETTER CHAIN BRACELET WITH JUMP RINGS

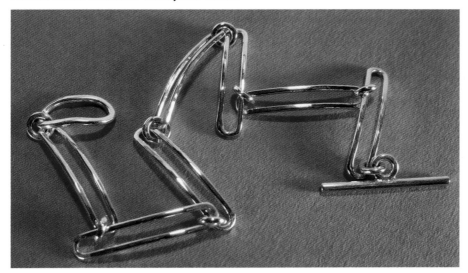

YOU WILL NEED:

♦ 1.3 mm (B&S 16) wire, cut into seven 55 mm (2¹/₈ in.) lengths
♦ Catch (see p.121)
♦ 1.3 mm (B&S 16) wire, for the jump rings, 150 mm (6 in.) long
♦ Strap hinge or similar
♦ Several blocks of plywood

The fetter chain consists of long links held together by jump rings. Fetters were originally used to restrain animals, and also humans, while allowing some freedom of movement. For the jewellery maker, the fetter link makes for the quick and easy creation of long lengths of chain, adds interest to a piece, and reduces the tedium of chain-making.

Each link in the example above is made from 1.3 mm (B&S 16) wire, 55 mm (2¹/₈ in.) long. There are seven links, each 26 mm (1 in.) long, and the overall length, including the catch, is 200 mm (8 in.). It will, of course, be easier to make this project from fewer longer links. Time is obviously saved when fewer links are needed, but not so obvious is the fact that a longer link is easier to forge and polish.

For this project use the same thickness of wire for the connecting jump rings as was used for the fetter links. The 1.3 mm (B&S 16) wire will create a strong link, and using the same thickness for both will give a uniform look to the work as a whole.

1. Begin by forming the seven rings that will form the fetter links, being especially careful to ensure a well-fitting joint. These soldered joints will have to withstand a good deal of force at the next stage of the process. (You may wish to refer to the ring-soldering section on p.36.) When all the joints are complete, make each ring roughly round on a ring mandrel, using a mallet.

2. Making the fetter links requires several simple devices. The first of these is a flat tapered punch about 2.5 mm thick, about 150 mm (6 in.) long and tapering from about 35 mm (1³/₈ in.) down to about 12 mm (¹/₂ in.). The one pictured right was made from the end of a strap hinge used to hang a gate. First, round off the corners by filing a chamfer on each edge. Then,

TIP   To accurately estimate the length of a finished bracelet, make sample links and keep a record of the length of wire used for each example.

first with a file, and then with emery cloth make all the edges completely smooth. Finally, polish the edges and faces.

3. The wooden block with the slot is made by sandwiching two strips of thin plywood between two pieces of hardwood or plywood. These are glued and screwed together, to create a slot that will allow the tapered punch to slide through it. The round stake is made from a piece of scaffolding pipe about 20 mm (¾ in.) wide, polished around one side. The scaffolding pipe, which is 48 mm (1⅞ in.) in diameter, provides just the right depth of curve for a bracelet link.

4. Each of the round links can now be shaped by placing them over the slot and hammering the tapered punch through them. Placing the join over the slot will ensure that the join is at the end of the link and, therefore, less visible. Take care not to test your joint too far. Having straightened the first link, you may like to put a mark on the tapered punch against the link, with a permanent pen. This will show the point on the punch that is not to be exceeded when stretching the rest of the links.

5. Next, bend each link with fingers or thumbs in a doming block, or alternatively use a soup spoon. With the scaffold-pipe stake held firmly in the vice, planish the face of each link.

6. Next place the link back on the tapered punch and, resting it on a flat stake or a hardwood block,

4a

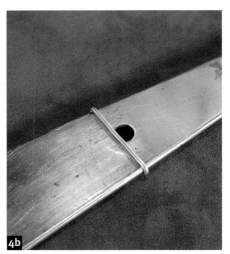

4b

5a

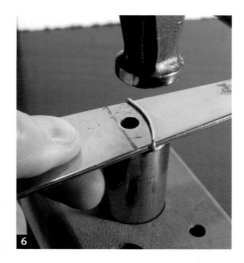

6

7

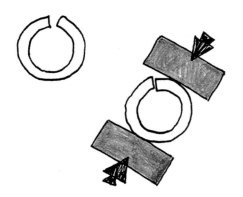

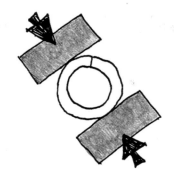

planish the edges and the ends. Try to create a more or less square section of wire. It is best, and safer, to polish all the links at this stage, before they are assembled.

7. To caluculate the size of jump ring needed place two fetter links touching each other end to end and measure the thickness with dividers. Add half a millimetre, then find a woodscrew with a shank of this size. It is difficult to be sure of the size by measuring in this way, so you may choose to make a model in copper or brass wire first. Alternatively, simply go ahead and make a batch of six or seven rings in silver. If they prove to be the wrong size, add them to your collection for use in future projects.

8. Planish each jump ring in the same way that the fetter links were planished. For this job, use a flat hammer or punch on a flat stake, as this will be less likely to open up the joint. Close any gaps that do form using the ends of a pair of pliers with the ring resting on a flat surface.

To open and close jump rings use two pairs of pliers and a twisting action.

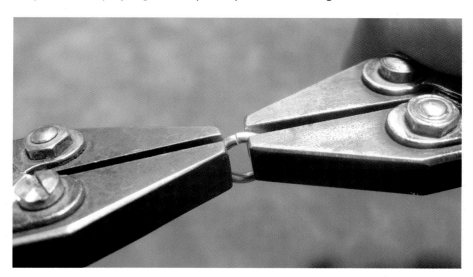

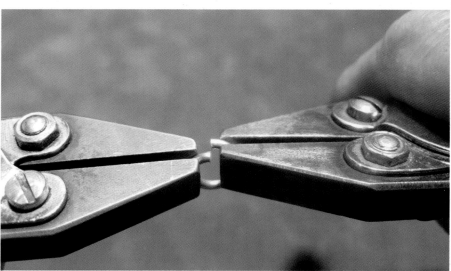

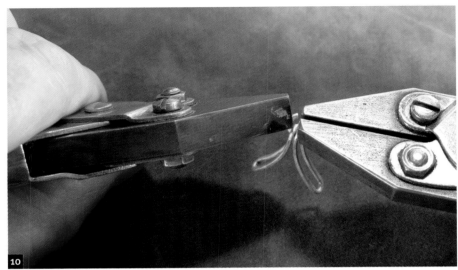

9. Thread each link in turn onto a tapered mandrel such as a knitting needle, and planish the edge to match the fetter links. Jump rings are best polished held on a ring, then finished on a polishing pad using a finger.

10. Assemble the links using two pairs of pliers, remembering to keep the fetter links back to back or face to face as you make the join, so that they face the same way when opened out. Always open and close a jump ring using a twisting action, rather than pulling the join apart. In this way the roundness of the ring is preserved.

Soldering jump rings in an assembled chain can present difficulties. The links either side can be softened by the heat. Oxides and fire stain can make subsequent polishing necessary, and there is a risk of inadvertently soldering separate links together.

In this project, it will not be necessary to solder the jump rings together, for three reasons: we have used thicker wire than is usually used for jump rings; we have made them as small in diameter as possible, reducing the leverage (the larger the diameter of the ring, the easier it will be to pull it open); and by planishing we have work-hardened the metal. The risk of these rings being pulled open in use is negligible.

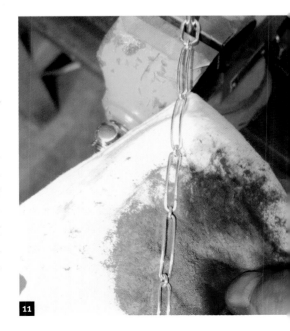

11. The assembled chain can now be given a final polish. Attach one end of the chain to the bench peg or a vice using a nail, and pull it tight with one hand. Use powdered rouge applied with a soft damp cloth, turning the chain over and reversing the ends to ensure that both ends and sides are polished evenly. Finally, the chain can be washed in soapy water using a soft brush. The use of powdered rouge rather than a block of rouge will prevent the build-up of polish and will therefore make this final process more effective.

FETTER CHAIN BRACELET WITHOUT JUMP RINGS

YOU WILL NEED:

- 1.2 mm (B&S 17) silver wire, about 450 mm (18 in.) long
- Curved T-bar catch (see p.122).
- 10 mm (³/₈ in.) dowel jig
- Mild steel, 1.5 mm thick and 80 mm (3¹/₈ in.) long
- Two strips of brass

An alternative fetter chain is one where all the links are fetter links with no jump rings in between. The links are shaped after they are joined, which makes it impossible to curve them so as to fit the wrist. For this reason the links have been made shorter.

1. Make a jig with a 10 mm (³/₈ in.) dowel; this will make links 17 mm (¹¹/₁₆ in.) long. Twelve are required to make a bracelet 200 mm (8 in.) long; 1.2 mm (B&S 17) wire has been used.

2. Solder five rings closed, then link two pairs together to make sets of three. Add an open ring to the remaining closed ring to make a pair. Join the two threes and the pair together to create a chain ten links long. Two open links remain for connecting the two parts of the catch to either end of the chain.

3. It will only be possible to polish this chain with all the links assembled, and polishing a chain presents special risks. To keep polishing to a minimum, prevent the formation of fire stain by making sure that all the links are thoroughly coated in flux before soldering.

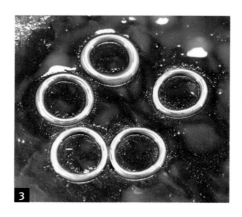

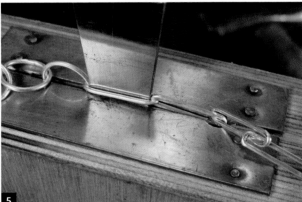

4. To forge the links to the required shape a new tapered punch will be needed. This one is made from 1.5 mm mild steel 80 mm (3$\frac{1}{8}$ in.) long, tapering from 20 mm ($\frac{3}{4}$ in.) down to 8 mm ($\frac{5}{16}$ in.). The edges are not completely rounded off, just the corners – leaving a flat edge. The whole surface must be thoroughly smoothed and polished.

The narrower slot required for this punch can be created on the underside of the the block used to make the last project (p.111) by nailing on two strips of brass to narrow the gap. (The hole at the end of the slot is to accommodate the T-bar when forming the end link).

5. Each link can now be forged to the shape of the punch with the link on either side of it, lying side-on in the slot. Try to ensure that the solder join is at one end. Planish the edges of each link while it is on the punch.

6. Planish the faces of the links on a flat stake.

7. Complete the assembly of the chain by soldering the remaining links to join the catches to either end of the chain. Forge these as for the rest of the links.

. . . .

TIP   TAKE EXTRA CARE WHEN POLISHING THE ASSEMBLED CHAIN. WORK ON EACH LINK INDIVIDUALLY WHILE KEEPING THE REST OF THE CHAIN WELL CLEAR OF THE POLISHING MOP.

. . . .

THE JIG-DESIGNED CHAIN

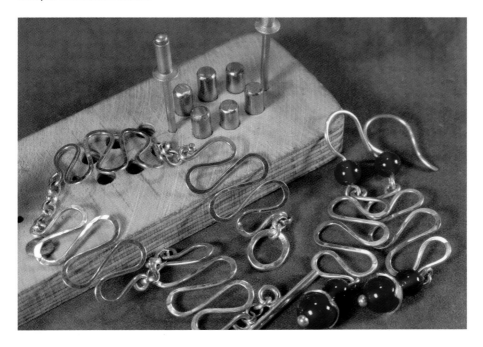

YOU WILL NEED:

◆ 1 mm (B&S 18) silver wire, about 600 mm (24 in.) long

◆ 12 mm (½ in.) plywood

◆ A four-inch nail (for the peg that is 4 mm in diameter)

◆ Two blind rivets

One of the great advantages of the fetter chain is that longer chains can be made from fewer links. Another way to achieve this is to make a feature of a link such as a scroll design, or a unit created with a jig. As well as ensuring that all the units are identical, a jig makes their construction easier. There is also the option of making matching pieces of jewellery – for example, a necklace or bracelet with matching earrings.

This jig is easy to make and uses easily found inexpensive materials. The design has no need of jump rings as the eyes at either end can be opened and closed in the same way as jump rings. It is used here with short lengths of chain to make a bracelet.

It is most important that the pegs are a good fit in the holes, loose enough to be pushed in and out easily with fingers, but not so loose as to fall out by themselves. Used as they are these nails are a very tight fit in holes of this size, so they must be reduced in diameter very slightly. The blind rivets fit easily into holes of 2 mm diameter.

1. Begin by drilling trial holes in the plywood, then, with a smooth file, emery paper and polishing machine, make the nails fit these holes. It is best to do this before you cut the pegs to length; a whole nail is much easier to handle than lots of short pieces. The pegs should be 20 mm (¾ in.) long. Make a little chamfer on each end, then give the pegs a final polish so that they slide easily into the holes. Remember, you may get a lot of use from this jig and its pegs, so it is worth getting them just right. Although you may make lots of jigs it is possible that the same pegs can be used on each.

TIP   DESIGNS SUCH AS THESE ARE USUALLY THE BETTER FOR HAVING AS FEW STRAIGHT SECTIONS AS POSSIBLE. AFTER THE UNIT IS REMOVED FROM THE JIG IT CAN BE ADJUSTED USING FINGERS WITHOUT CHANGING THE BASIC SHAPE.

TIP   THERE MUST ALWAYS BE ENOUGH SPACE BETWEEN EACH PEG TO ALLOW THE WIRE TO WRAP AROUND BOTH PEGS.

Expect to make lots of jigs, as the only way to judge their effectiveness is by trial and error. Use copper or brass wire to test each one, and finish each sample by planishing, to properly test the effectiveness of the design. Small changes can make a big difference to the look of this kind of work.

2. To make the design shown, begin by making the end of the wire square, then, with the tip of the round-nosed pliers, bend the end around until it meets the side to form the eye. Use the end of the jaws in every case to make sure the units are identical. Secure this eye to the first hole using the blind rivet, then, with all the pegs of the jig pushed down, wind the wire around each peg in turn, pushing each one up from underneath as required.

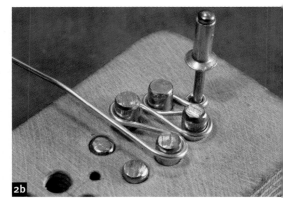

3. The last stage is to bend the wire around the blind rivet at the end. Snip off the waste with end cutters and push the end against the side of the wire to form the eye.

4. Since this design is not soldered, it must be stiffened to prevent its being pulled out of shape. Planishing will harden the metal, and the change in the profile of the wire will help to preserve its shape. The appearance of the work is also enhanced by the hammer marks that enliven the surface.

First hollow the unit by pressing it with your fingers into a doming block or a soup spoon. On a slightly domed stake, cover the whole piece with hammer marks, then concentrate the hammer on the outside of the bends. This will help to fix the shape, and the difference it creates in the width of the wire will add interest to the piece.

TIP   AVOID PLANISHING THE EYES AT EITHER END, AS THIS WILL MAKE THEM MORE DIFFICULT TO OPEN AND CLOSE.

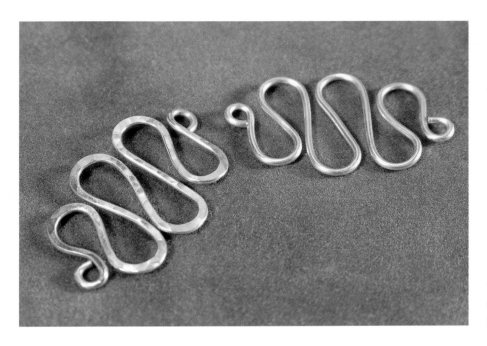

The effect of planishing the wire can be seen here: the piece on the left has been planished; the piece on the right has not.

OVAL LINK CHAIN

The links on this chain are made using an oval nail as a former. Any of the links can be used as one half of the toggle catch (see p.122), so that the bracelet can be made to fit several different sizes of wrist.

YOU WILL NEED:

♦ 1.2 mm (B&S 17) silver wire, about half a metre (20 in.) long

♦ 1 mm (BS 19) silver wire, about 250 mm (10 in.) long, for the jump rings

♦ Bead

♦ Curved T-bar catch (see p.122).

♦ Six-inch oval nail

♦ Small block of wood

♦ 1 mm (BS 19) Silver sheet for octagonal cap (see p.136)

1. Take a six-inch oval nail and, using a grindstone, files and emery paper, form the end into a gradual taper. Polish the whole nail including the parallel section. This nail mandrel should measure 7 x 5 mm in section.

2. Saw the large links on a 6 mm (¼ in.) former (see p.109). There are 20 in this example. Solder all the links closed, forge each link into an oval by hammering the nail mandrel through the links into a 7 mm hole. To protect the edge of the hole, you may like to use a 6 mm (¼ in.) washer that has been opened out into an oval with a needle file and then polished. In this example a hole has been punched in a strip of brass and rolled out into an oval.

3. Planish the edges of the links on the nail mandrel, then the faces on a stake. When all planishing is complete, thread the links onto the nail to polish the edges. This stage of the polishing process is made easier by the fact that the links are unable to spin around on the oval mandrel. Polish the faces with each link held by wire or string. The jump rings are made from 1 mm (B&S 18) wire on a 3 mm (⅛ in.) former; these must be planished and polished before assembly.

4. Connect all the links, then examine each link for burrs and remove them with a smooth file or an emery board. Polish the completed chain with powdered rouge on a soft cloth.

5. The bead at the end is mounted on 1 mm (B&S 18) wire with a silver bead and a small octagonal cap (see p.136). There is an extra jump ring between the T-bar and the last link in the chain, to ensure that there is plenty of room to thread the T-bar into the chosen link. (See p.122 for how to make a T-bar catch.)

CATCHES

THE T-BAR OR TOGGLE CATCH

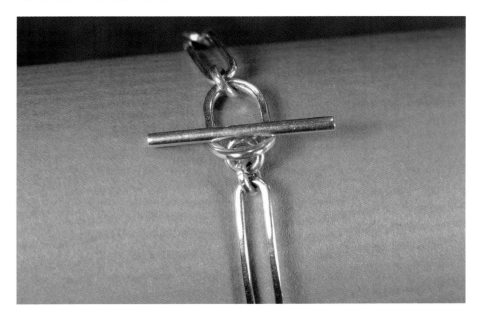

The T-bar is pushed through a hole or ring end on, then lies sideways in slight tension across the hole to secure a bracelet or necklace. All that is needed is a bar with a loose fixing in the centre to allow it to be connected to the end of a chain. This example is used with the fetter chain.

1. This T-bar is made from 2 mm (B&S 14) round wire and a jump ring made from wire of the same size as has been used in the rest of the chain. Cut a length of wire to about 35 mm (1³⁄₈ in.) and straighten it by lightly planishing it as it is rolled across a flat stake.

2. Place a pallion of easy solder halfway along its length and heat it until the solder melts.

3. Close the jump ring and solder the join with a little more solder than you would normally use. The aim is to create a swelling of solder across the join. Holding the ring in a vice or with pliers, file a flat on this lump of solder against the join.

4. File a slight groove on the edge of your soldering block or charcoal to allow the 2 mm wire to sit just lower than the surface so that the centre of the bar is level with the centre of the jump ring.

3

5. Flux both pieces and place them alongside each other so that the centre of the smaller jump ring is opposite the centre of the thicker bar.

6. Reheat the work, beginning with the thicker bar, until you see the solder melt and draw the two parts together.

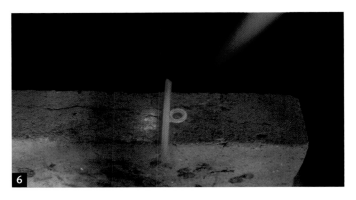

7. The T-bar can now be trimmed to make both sides equal, and the ends rounded off and polished. The block of wood used as a guide is held in a vice to leave both hands free to hold the work and the cutters.

8. The small link through which the T-bar passes is made from 1.5 mm (B&S 15) silver wire 40 mm (1½ in.) long. After soldering, make it round on a mandrel, and then squeeze it slightly using pliers or a vice to create flat sides. Planish it on the scaffold-pipe stake to match the other parts, polish, then connect it to the chain with a jump ring.

CURVED T-BAR

YOU WILL NEED:

♦ 1.8 mm (B&S 13) wire 30 mm (1⅛ in.) long (for the bar)

♦ 1 mm wire (B&S 18) which has been formed around a 3 mm (⅛ in.) rod (for the jump ring)

♦ 1.3 mm (B&S 16) wire, 40 mm (1⅝ in.) long (for the ring at the other end.

This T-bar has been curved and tapered to make it more secure. The anchor-like form seems an appropriate shape for a fastening device, and can be made slightly smaller than if it were straight.

1. To make a curved T-bar, follow the instructions for making a straight T-bar, but after soldering, trim the ends of the T-bar with end cutters to 12 mm (½ in.) from the edge of the jump ring.

2. Bend the work around a dowel of broom-handle size, or a cylindrical stake of 25 mm (1 in.), that has been drilled to accommodate the jump ring. You may need to use a mallet to do this.

3. Forge the centre section down to the thickness of the jump ring, turning the work over and working from both sides to keep it symmetrical.

4. Each end of the bar can now be forged at right angles to the line of the jump ring. Begin by making a fishtail shape on each end, then work back towards the middle to create a gradual taper. The midpoints between the ends and the centre should be roughly square in section. For this process a small round stake is useful; alternatively use the side of the 25 mm (1 in.) stake drilled with a hole to accommodate the jump ring.

5. File the ends to a rounded shape and then polish.

6. The ring at the other end of the bracelet is made of 1.3 mm (B&S 16) wire and is formed around a 6.5 mm (¼ in.) dowel. After soldering, squeeze it in a vice or with pliers to make it slightly oval, then hollow in a swage block, planish and then polish.

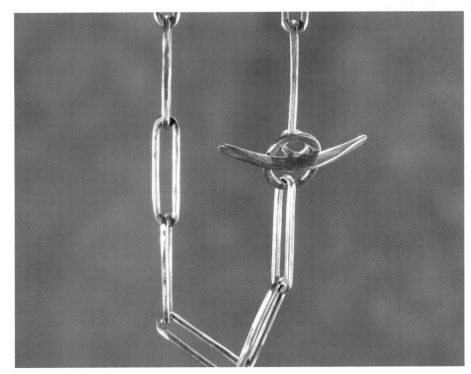

C-CATCH VERSION 1

A catch is sometimes more than just a functional closure; it can be regarded as a decorative object in its own right. Instead of the necklace being joined at the back of the neck, the catch can be displayed at the front for all to see.

The C-catch, whether it is made in wire or from sheet material, depends for its effectiveness and security on being slightly difficult to uncouple. Making the 'C' longer in one direction, with the cut on the longer side, ensures that it hangs with the joints apart from each other. To couple and uncouple this catch the grooves must be both opposite and at right angles to each other.

YOU WILL NEED:

♦ 1.8 mm (B&S 13) silver wire, 80 mm (¾ in.) long

♦ Six-inch oval nail (to use as a former)

One end of the link must be wide enough for a small hole.

1. Make two links on a 6 mm (¼ in.) former and solder them closed. Forge both to the oval shape on the nail mandrel, then flatten them on a flat stake. In this version the two ellipses have been forged thinner and wider at one end to make room for a 1.5 mm hole. It can now be drilled and countersunk using the nail punch, and the gap finished with a needle file and polished.

2. Using end cutters, make a cut about halfway down one long side. Be careful not to cut too deep, just far enough to make a groove to provide a location for the chisel. There will, of course, be a second, matching groove on the opposing side.

3. Make the chisel from a four-inch oval nail. Grind and file the end into a chisel point, the angle of which should be a little greater than 90 degrees. Locate the chisel in the groove and tap it gently, then turn the work over and do the same to the other side. Continue this process until there are two grooves of equal depth with little metal left between them.

4. Cut through this remaining metal using shears or side cutters. The gap can now be finished with a needle file and polished to remove any burrs.

C-CATCH VERSION 2

This version of the C-catch uses a combination of silver and bronze. Both metals have been rolled to apply an identical pattern. The blanks from the punched holes have been used as links. The contrast between the two halves of the catch will be enhanced as the piece ages and the bronze develops a patina.

YOU WILL NEED:

♦ 0.8 mm (B&S 20) silver sheet, 27 x 27 mm (1 x 1 in.)
♦ 0.8 mm (B&S 20) bronze sheet, 27 x 27 mm (1 x 1 in.)

1. Begin by cutting out two discs approximately 25 mm (1 in.) in diameter. Punch a 10 mm (³/₈ in.) hole in the centre of each one. When cutting outside curves with shears, it is best to cut outside the line to begin with. Punch the hole at this stage then, if the hole is not exactly in the centre, as sometimes happens, an adjustment can be made to the final outside cut.

2. Anneal both discs, replace the centres, wrap both in a suitable embossing material and pass them through the rolling mill. All parts of the work will now have an identical pattern on both sides and will have been equally distorted into ellipses.

3. Drill the 1.5 mm holes and finish these with the nail punch. Bevel all the edges by planishing, with the hammer overlapping the edge of the work.

4. Finally, make the cuts along each long side using cutters and a chisel, and finish with needle files and polish. Assemble the four components, with the bronze disc connected to the silver side of the catch and the silver disc to the bronze.

THE BOLT RING

A bolt ring is one of the most widely used catches, being secure, fairly easy to open and close, and available in a wide variety of sizes. The catch featured in this section, although not strictly a bolt ring, uses the same principal, and is made using this simple device. This is a smaller version of the ring-swaging device on p.84, a 16 mm (⅝ in.) round bar, drilled to fit an M6 (¼ in.) bolt and chamfered to 45 degrees.

YOU WILL NEED:

♦ A short length of 1.5 mm (B&S 15) silver wire

♦ A short length of 1 mm (B&S 18) silver wire

♦ 0.5 mm (B&S 24) silver sheet, 3 mm (⅛ in.) wide

♦ A ring swaging device (see above)

1. Begin by making a ring of 1.5 mm (B&S 15) wire, about 10 mm (⅜ in.) in diameter. Flatten this ring to make it about 1 mm thick, and file a small groove where the solder join is, in case it is hard to find after the planishing process.

2. Make a jump ring of 1 mm (B&S 18) wire and solder it to the larger ring at a point just alongside the solder joint on the larger ring.

The finished ring in the open and closed position.

3. Make a little ring to fit the inside of this flat ring, using 0.5 mm (B&S 24) silver 3 mm ($\frac{1}{8}$ in.) wide. Use pi to establish the length of silver required. Err on the small side then planish this ring until it fits snugly inside the flat ring. Anneal the inside ring then line up the solder joins on both rings and thread the assembled pieces onto the bolt. As the nut is tightened on the bolt, the little ring is forced out around the flat ring to make it captive. Saw through both rings together, either side of the joins, to leave a gap of about 2 mm.

4. Round off the sharp edges of both rings with needle files and emery boards, and by polishing. It will now be possible to twist the captive inner ring around, within the outer ring, to open and close the gap.

BOLT RING PENDANT

An alternative method to construct this catch is to punch out a hole in a sheet of metal. The inner ring is made to fit the hole, then swaged and sawn through as before. The same swaging tool has been used in the example illustrated: the punched hole is 8 mm ($\frac{5}{16}$ in.) diameter; the silver has been hollowed slightly and planished, and holes have been drilled along the bottom edge to hold hanging beads. The planishing is, of course, carried out after the drilling of the holes and before the swaging of the inner ring. The catch forms the centrepiece of a necklace of fetter links.

YOU WILL NEED:

- 0.8 mm (B&S 20) sheet silver, 31 x 31 mm
- A swaging tool (see above)
- Block of wood
- A 4-inch round nail
- Beads and a 6 mm (¼ in.) cabochon
- A short length of chain.

1. Begin by making a paper template using compasses set to 30 mm ($1\frac{1}{8}$ in.). This can then be positioned on the silver sheet to create as little waste as possible. Using a centre punch and dividers, mark out the shape and cut it out using shears or with a piercing saw.

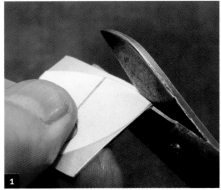

2. Mark the position of the 10 mm (³/₈ in.) hole against a centre line using a permanent pen. Fasten it carefully in the die and punch out the hole. An alternative to the use of a punch and die is to drill a pilot hole, then pierce out the hole with a piercing saw.

TIP   HOLES OF THIS SIZE SHOULD NEVER BE DRILLED USING A LARGE DRILL. THE RESULTING HOLE IS ALWAYS UNTIDY AND THERE IS A RISK OF THE DRILL JAMMING IN THE THIN SHEET. THE LITTLE DISC OF METAL CREATED BY PUNCHING OR PIERCING, AS COMPARED TO THE SWARF FROM THE LARGE DRILL, CAN USUALLY BE PUT TO SOME USE.

3. Mark out, centre-punch and drill the 1.5 mm holes, then remove the burrs with a larger drill. An effective finish can be created on small holes like these using a simple punching system. Take a four-inch round nail, saw off the point and, using a grindstone, file, emery boards, and a polishing machine, make a small, smooth dome on the end. Holding the nail in the chuck of an electric drill can make this task a little easier.

4. Drill a 4.5 mm hole in a block of hardwood or thick plywood and knock in the nail until the little dome is just proud of the surface of the wood. Saw off the nail and file what remains until it is flush with the underside of the wood. Repeat the process with the rest of the nail to create the punch, and drill a 5 mm hole in the wood in which to store it. Both sides of the small holes can now be embellished at once. This not only improves the appearance of the work, but also hardens the metal around the hole. The hangers are suspended from short lengths of chain, using the smallest of jump rings.

5. The fetter chain has been made with links of three different lengths. Instead of jump rings, haematite beads mounted on 1 mm (B&S 18) silver wire are used. Each eye has been flattened using a polished punch while resting on a little anvil. Drill a hole in a strip of steel and polish all around it; the hole should be slightly larger than the bead. Resting the work on this simple device leaves the hands free to hold both hammer and punch.

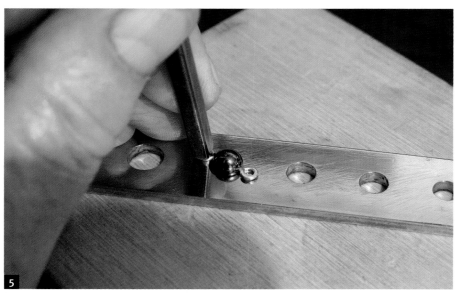

CORD FOR NECKLACES

Some of the earliest, most primitive jewellery was made of beads, usually of horn or bone, threaded onto a cord. The use of cord – be it silk, cotton or especially leather – is still a useful option for the modern jeweller. These materials are not only less expensive than most metals, but are often better suited to particular designs; a chain of silver, for example, can be a distraction when used to support a simple, informal pendant. No metalworking skills are required; just find suitable beads and an appropriate cord, and tie the right knots.

The right knot can be more than just a matter of practical use. Knots have been used in jewellery-making for thousands of years and are often rich in meaning and symbolism. These things should not be ignored in the design of jewellery, which has so many sentimental associations.

THE SLIPKNOT NECKLACE

Make your selection of beads and thread them onto a length of cord, in this case 1 mm leather. Tie a loose overhand knot on one end of the cord, and pass the other end of the cord through it. Tighten the knot just enough to allow the cord to slip through it to form a noose. Draw the noose to the size which will pass easily over the wearer's head. Tie the loose end of the cord to the far side of the first knot, using the same overhand knot.

It will now be possible to pull on each knotted end, to shorten the necklace, leaving the knots lying at either side of the neck. A knot tied on each end after the slipknot will prevent the cord from slipping through the fingers.

The slipknot system can, of course, be used back to front, the double section of the cord passing through the pendant so that the slipknots lie out of sight at the back of the neck. In the example pictured at the top of the page both strands have been threaded with beads.

A slipknot.

An alternative slipknot using a bead.

This kind of work can be confusing, so practise first with string; one end of this length has been dyed to make it easier to see how the system works.

As an alternative to the slipknot, a bead with a hole just large enough for two thicknesses of cord can be used as a tightening device. Check the hole in the bead carefully, as any sharp corners can damage the cord. Fine carborundum grit on a piece of string can be used to make the hole smooth.

OTHER KNOTS

The figure-of-eight knot, above, (known alternatively as the Savoy knot or the lover's knot) is used in heraldry as a symbol of faithfulness. To tie this knot, form a loop in the cord, wrap the loose end around the cord below the loop, then pass it through the loop from the top.

An alternative way of combining beads and cord is this design (right) where the beads hang vertically. Choose the beads, and then make a ring in silver just large enough to allow the largest bead to pass through. Tie a loose knot on the end of a one-metre (three-foot) length of cord, thread on the beads, and loosely tie off the other end. Fold the cord double and fasten it to the silver ring at its midpoint using a simple hitch knot. Instead of the silver ring a loop can be made in the cord itself, though this may be too plain and simple.

Each end with its beads can be passed through the ring separately to form the necklace. Once you have decided on the correct length of cord, the knots can be made permanent. As this forms the focal point of the necklace, a basic overhand knot is a bit too plain, so here a blood knot is used.

As these examples show, this design of necklace offers many possibilities for variation in the style of silver ring and the way it is used.

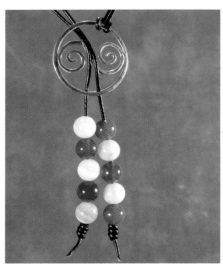
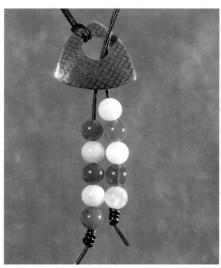

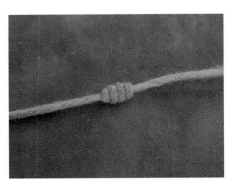

The blood knot (above) is so called because it was tied on each of the nine ends of the cat-o'-nine-tails. The blood knot was also used by friars of the strict Capuchin order, as a simple way to add weight to the ends of the rope around their habits. A more mundane name for this knot is the multiple overhand knot.

To make a blood knot, begin with an overhand knot, then continue passing the end of the cord through the loop, three or four times. As it is drawn tight, both ends of the knot must be pulled with the fingers towards the middle, to form neat symmetrical coils. Leave at least 10 mm (3/8 in.) of cord beyond the knot to make it secure, and to show off its symmetry.

LEATHER CORD WITH METAL FINDINGS

Although a knotted leather cord is quite satisfactory as a necklace, there are times when a metal catch or link is a more sensible option. A knot tied in thick cord, for example, can be rather clumsy, and metal and leather used in combination can often be more attractive. Sometimes a belt needs its silver buckle.

The problem of joining a metal catch to leather cord presents the jewellery maker an opportunity for innovation. One solution to the problem is to use chenier, thin silver tubing, which can be fixed to the cord using pliers or a vice.

Chenier can be made using a drawplate, can be bought in a wide variety of sizes, and can be made in short lengths on the removable spindle tool (see p.107).

Cut off a 12 mm (1/2 in.) length of chenier. Here a jig has been used. This makes it easier to make the pieces all the same length and also holds the small pieces for finishing. Thread the chenier onto each end of

the cord, and insert a little epoxy resin for extra securrity. Squeeze the last 4 mm in a vice, but be careful not to squeeze too tight and crush the cord. Drill a hole in each of the flattened ends and insert a jump ring.

An alternative method of joining leather cord to a silver catch is to use short lengths of silver chain. Simply thread the cord through the links, being sure to pass it through in the same direction each time. Join the jump ring and the catch to the last link in the chain. This method, although it can only be used with thin flexible cord, will make a neat and tidy connection which is easy to make, secure, and can, if necessary, be undone.

EARRINGS

EAR WIRES

There are two main methods of securing jewellery to earlobes. The first requires that the earlobe be pierced, and the second makes use of springs, screws and other mechanisms, all of which are beyond the scope of this book.

Wires for pierced ears can be divided into the hook, and the peg and scroll forms. The peg, with its tiny groove, and the scroll, which secures it, are marvels of machine-made jewellery, produced for remarkably little cost.

Three different types of ear wire.

For reasons of cost, as well as the level of difficulty in its making and the fact that it is rarely seen in use (being hidden behind the ear), the peg-and-scroll means of fastening is also beyond our scope. This leaves just the hook, sometimes called the shepherd's crook ear wire.

The wire used should be slightly thinner than 1 mm (B&S 18): no thinner than 0.8 mm (B&S 20) but no more than 0.9 mm (B&S 19). Too thin and the hook may be uncomfortable, but too thick and it may be difficult to insert into the pierced earlobe and may also look clumsy. Bear in mind that the hook will always be strong enough, as earrings need to be light in weight for comfort's sake.

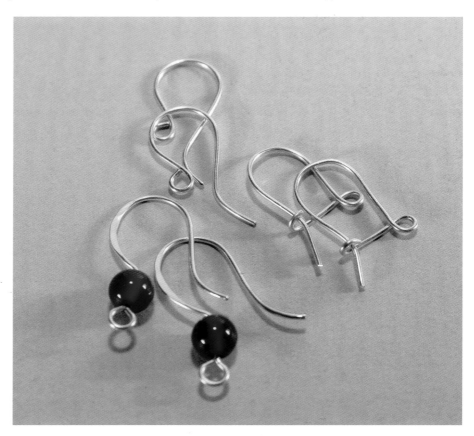

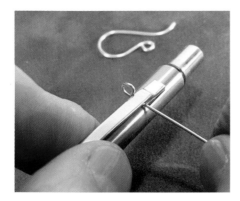  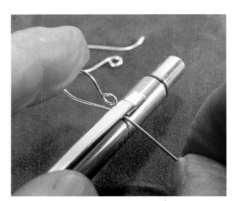

Simple yet effective hooks can be made using round-nosed pliers and a propelling pencil. The pencil must have a clip to secure it to a pocket. Begin by forming an eye on the end of the wire with round-nosed pliers. Use the end of the jaws to ensure that they are exactly the same on each wire. Thread the wire through the clip, with the eye resting against the clip, then wrap the wire around the pencil until the wire touches the eye.

Slide it out from under the clip, turn it over, then thread it under the clip again. With the other side of the eye resting against the clip, make the final bend. You may choose to use a larger-diameter pen top for this bend. You can, of course, do all of this work with round-nosed pliers, but the use of a former, even though it is just a pencil, makes it easier to make a matching pair – indeed, as many matching pairs as you need.

The next design has the advantage that it can be locked. To make it will involve the creation of a simple plywood or MDF jig. The holes are 8 mm ($^5/_{16}$ in.) and 2 mm at 15 mm ($^5/_8$ in.) centres. The two small holes are at 9 mm centres. There is a 1 mm blind hole about 5 mm ($^3/_{16}$ in.) deep, to secure the end of the wire at the start. The 8 mm ($^5/_{16}$ in.) peg is 20 mm ($^3/_4$ in.) long, and blind rivets are used in the small holes (see drawing opposite, top left).

Push the end of a length of wire into the blind hole, fold it flat and wrap it around each peg in turn, pulling tight at each bend. Cut off the loose end

at a point mid-way between the two blind rivets. Release it from the jig and trim off the bent section at the other end. With two pairs of pliers, twist the end through 90 degrees to form the hook (see pictue on p.133). A small emery board is useful to round off and smooth the ends of ear wires.

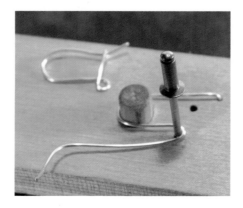 

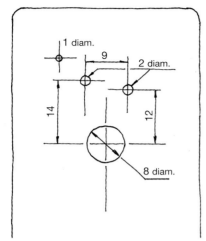

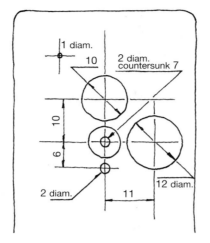

**Measurements for earwire jig.
All dimensions are in mm.**

The final ear-wire design incorporates a bead which matches those on the drop earrings. This illustrates another advantage of making findings, even ear wires, which otherwise offer little scope for originality. The jig is again made of plywood with dowels of 10 mm ($^3/_8$ in.) and 12 mm ($^1/_2$in.) diameter. There is also a blind hole and a countersunk hole to accommodate the bead.

The eye on this design has been made symmetrical. To do this, make the end of the wire square and make a bend at right angles using the blind hole as a guide to its length, then use the end of the round-nosed pliers to form the eye (see p.83). With this method of forming an eye the depth of the hole, and the size of the jaws of the pliers, can only be arrived at by trial and error; in this example the hole was 10 mm ($^3/_8$ in.) deep.

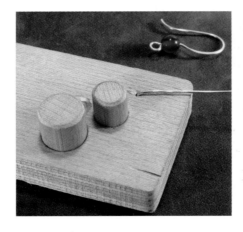

With the eye firmly held in a vice or with pliers, thread on the bead and bend the wire at right angles in line with the eye. Secure the eye to the first hole in the jig using a blind rivet, and with the bead pressed into the countersunk hole, bend the wire around the 10 mm ($^3/_8$ in.) dowel until it touches the bead. Push the large dowel into place and make the final bend around it. After trimming to size and rounding off the end, you may want to flatten the wire alongside the bead. This will lessen the chance of its being bent out of shape in use.

EARRING DESIGNS

Uniquely among jewellery, ear decoration, with the exception of studs, is susceptible to the effects of movement and the play of light. All drop-earring designs should take account of this effect, whether by using translucent or faceted stones, plique-a-jour enamel, or the many techniques for applying surface texture to metal. Links should be as loose as possible, to allow more freedom of movement and the maximum light reflection.

YOU WILL NEED:

◆ Two 8 mm diameter beads

◆ Two 6 mm (¼ in.) diameter beads

◆ 0.5 mm (B&S 24) silver sheet, cut into two squares 9 x 9 mm

◆ 8 mm dowel

◆ Two pieces of 1 mm (B&S 18) silver wire, each about 100 mm (4 in.) long

JIG-DESIGNED EARRINGS

This design uses a link from the bracelet on p.117. The 8 mm (⁵/₁₆ in.) bead, with its little cap, and the 6 mm (¼ in.) bead above it encourage movement and help to show off the faceted surface of the link.

1. The caps are made from 0.5 mm silver, 9 mm (³/₈ in.) square. Make a strip of silver and drill the 1 mm holes before cutting each little square to length. Polish all the edges, and then form the domes in the doming block.

2. Some minor damage may be done to the dome in the doming block, but this is easily repaired by mounting the dome on a length of dowel. Round off the end of an 8 mm dowel and drill a 1 mm hole in the end to take a pin. Held in this way it will be easier to finish it with emery boards and polishing machine. Polish away from the pin towards the edges.

3. The tiny silver bead at the end of the wire is not part of the original wire. Balling up the end of a length of wire will not create the right shape of bead and there may be some weakening of the metal around the melted section. This bead is made separately and sweated onto the squared-off end of the wire. Make each bead from an identical length of wire to ensure that the beads are exactly the same size.

Make a little hollow in the firebrick or charcoal with a drill. Rest the bead upside down in the hollow and melt a pallion of solder onto it. Bend the wire into a triangular shape so that the end rests vertically on the bead, and reheat. Concentrate the flame on the bead, to avoid melting the thin wire, until the solder re-melts and the join is made.

4. Thread the 8 mm bead and the 6 mm bead onto the wire, and form an eye on the end of the wire.

FORGED LINK EARRINGS

1. This design uses forged links. Begin by forging a flat on one end of the 2.5 mm (B&S 10) wire to create a kind of fishtail shape. Extend this flat to just beyond the halfway point on the wire, making lighter blows as the halfway point is reached. The aim is to make a gradual transition from flat to round. Use a rounded stake and hammer, which will help to swell the ends to a wider shape.

2. Turn the wire through 90 degrees, then repeat the process on the other end of the wire. Holding the flattened end with pliers rather than fingers will make it easier to judge whether it is being held at right angles to the end being worked on. The finished unit should be flat at either end but square in section at the midpoint. It will also be 5–10 mm longer than its original length.

TIP   IF THE HAMMER FAVOURS ONE SIDE OF THE WORK, THAT SIDE WILL BECOME THINNER AND THEREFORE LONGER, CAUSING THE WIRE TO BEND. TO KEEP THE WORK STRAIGHT AND OF AN EVEN THICKNESS, ALWAYS DIRECT THE HAMMER TO THE INSIDE OF THE BEND.

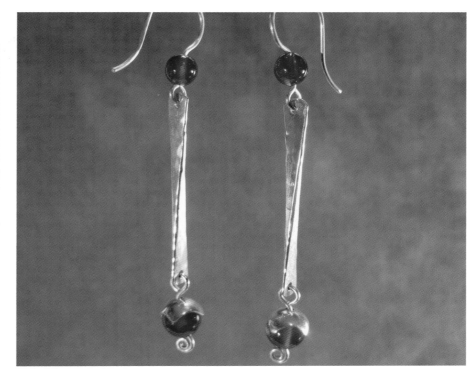

1a

1b

2a

2b

3. Complete the forging on a flat stake, turning the work over repeatedly until the symmetrical shape is achieved. Avoid finishing with emery boards, but polish the work directly after planishing to preserve the hammer marks.

4. Trim the ends to make them square and drill each end with a 1.5 mm hole. This will ensure plenty of clearance around the 1 mm (B&S 18) wire rings, and allow them to swing freely. The 8 mm ($^5/_{16}$ in.) bead with its silver cap hanging from the forging will also encourage movement.

5. The bead is mounted on a length of 0.8 mm (B&S 20) wire. File a taper on the end of the wire, then using the tip of the round-nosed pliers, form the little scroll. Hold the wire securely with the pliers, then bend the scroll until the wire is in line with the centre of the scroll. Hold the scroll in a vice or with pliers, and thread on the bead and its cap.

6. Cut the wire to length – there should be 10 mm ($^3/_8$ in.) above the cap – and file the end smooth. Bend the wire over in line with the little scroll, and form the eye using round-nosed pliers.

EARRING DESIGNS: CHAINS

The large chain links in these designs (below and opposite above) allow as much free movement as possible. There will always be a polished surface facing to the front and to the side. Planishing is used to create lively surfaces.

The earrings pictured to the right are made of eight rings of three different sizes, in this case, 10, 15 and 20 mm. Precise sizes are not important and the little chain can be assembled at random, not necessarily as matching pairs. Each ring has been planished.

TIP MAKING A MODEL OF THE WIRE SECTION IN COPPER IS A GOOD IDEA; THIS WILL HELP TO ENSURE THE CREATION OF THE ALL-IMPORTANT MATCHING PAIR.

The next design (opposite, above right) is also a chain but slightly more complicated. In each earring there are four large rings, 20 mm ($^3/_4$ in.) in diameter, and four small rings of about 6 mm ($^1/_4$ in.) diameter. In order to distinguish one from another, we shall call the small ring a link, and the large ring a hoop.

1. Begin by making the small chain, using 1.2 mm (B&S 13) wire around a 6 mm ($^1/_4$ in.) former (see p.109). When soldering links in a chain, it is important to keep previous joints apart to prevent the accidental joining of links. One way to do this

YOU WILL NEED:

♦ A length of 1.2 mm (B&S 17) wire, about 150 mm long

♦ Eight strips of 1.5 mm (B&S 15) wire, 65 mm (2½ in.) long

♦ Two ear wires (see p.133)

is to hold the link being soldered in locked tweezers, against a firebrick. The links you want to protect hang safely beneath the heat.

2. Planish each link, using a small stake, and polish.

3. Make the hoops from 1.5 mm (B&S 15) wire, 63 mm (2½ in.) long, and thread them in order onto the chain, with the first large hoop through the top link. If the proportions are correct, the small chain should fit within the first hoop. Bear in mind that planishing will stretch the hoops.

4. The second hoop goes through the first hoop, as well as the second link. The next hoop passes through the third link and both hoops. Finally, the bottom hoop is threaded through the last link and all three of the hoops. As you thread the second, third and fourth hoops, check that each hangs correctly before you solder them closed. Each hoop should lie at right angles to the one above it.

5. The large hoops can now be made round, planished and polished to complete the project.

This project has a charming and unexpected quality. The planished silver makes a tinkling sound with each movement of the wearer's head. Surprises like this add to the joys of jewellery making.

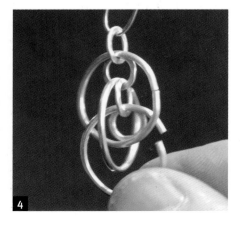

Ring sizing table

RING SIZE (UK, IRELAND, AUSTRALIA)	LENGTH OF METAL REQUIRED (MM)
A	37.5
B	39
C	40.2
D	41.4
E	42.6
F	43.8
G	45
H	46.2
I	47.4
J	48.6
K	49.8
L	51
M	52.2
N	53.5
O	54.7
P	56
Q	57.3
R	58.6
S	59.9
T	61.1
U	62.4
V	63.7
W	64.9
X	66.1
Y	67.3
Z	68.5

Wire sizing table

B&S GAUGE NUMBER	DIAMETER (MM.)	DIAMETER (IN.)
30	0.2548	0.01003
29	0.2845	0.01120
28	0.3211	0.01264
27	0.3607	0.01420
26	0.4049	0.01594
25	0.4547	0.01790
24	0.5105	0.02010
23	0.5733	0.02257
22	0.6439	0.02535
21	0.7229	0.02846
20	0.8118	0.03196
19	0.9116	0.03589
18	1.024	0.04030
17	1.150	0.04526
16	1.291	0.05082
15	1.450	0.05707
14	1.628	0.06408
13	1.828	0.07196
12	2.053	0.08081
11	2.305	0.09074
10	2.588	0.1019

Glossary

abrading wearing down material using an abrasive such as *emery paper*, Carborundum grit or *Water of Ayr* stone.

acrylic thermoplastic material that softens when heated.

alloy a mixture of metals; brass, for example, is made of copper and zinc. Gold is usually alloyed with other metals such as silver or copper to improve its working properties and also to change its colour.

annealing softening metal by heating. See *work hardening*.

bail connecting device, usually used to hang a pendant.

barette file a pointed file with a smooth back and smooth sloping edges.

bevel sloping surface applied to the edge of a flat sheet, usually with a hammer.

bezel thin metal ring that holds a cabochon in place. The cabochon is placed inside the bezel and the thin metal is pushed over the stone with a pusher. This is sometimes called a rub-over setting.

blank a piece of wire or sheet metal cut to size. The raw material for a project.

bodkin a metal rod, tapering to a point, usually having a wooden handle.

bolt ring circular catch made from fine tubing with a wire ring inside it, which can be twisted to open and close.

borax a flux used during soldering. Borax usually comes in solid form shaped as a cone, and is ground on a slate dish and water added to make a solution with a milk-like consistency.

bending jig device usually made of wood, with holes into which fit pegs, used to bend wire accurately.

burnisher highly polished steel or agate tool that is rubbed against softer metal to make it harder and to impart a polish.

burr rough edge created by filing or drilling. Burrs must be removed with care to avoid scratching the surrounding area.

cabochon ground and polished semi precious stone. It is usually round or oval and domed to fit in a bezel setting.

chamfer a sloping surface at an edge or corner.

chasing surface decoration of metal made using punches, working on the front only. See *repoussé*.

chenier fine tubing made using the draw plate, used in making findings and also hinges.

countersink to enlarge the upper part of a hole so that the head of a screw or a rivet can sit below the surface. A countersink can also be used to embellish a hole and to harden the surrounding metal.

cutters tools used to cut wire. Unlike shears, which act like scissors, their jaws come together opposite one another. Side cutters work like a pair of pliers, and end cutters like pincers.

dividers tool like a pair of compasses with two points, that is used to scribe arcs and circles on sheet metal, or a line parallel to an edge.

doming block brass or steel block with hollows of different sizes, used with punches of wood or metal to force metal into dome shapes.

draw filing method of smoothing an edge by drawing a file along the edge at right angles to it.

emery paper abrasive material, usually glued to boards or sticks. The higher the grade number, the finer the grit. Only the finest grades are used in jewellery making.

findings fixings such as clasps, pins and ear wires. In former times a jeweller would 'find' a suitable piece of metal from among his scraps and off-cuts.

fire brick heat resistant material on which metal is heated.

firestain surface film caused by oxidisation that remains on sterling silver after firing. Firestain can be prevented by the use of flux or must be removed by abrading and polishing.

flux substance applied to metal before soldering. During heating, flux forms a protective layer, which prevents the formation of surface oxides and allows the solder to flow.

forging shaping metal using hammers. Forging differs from planishing in that the form is changed quite considerably; planishing is a surface treatment.

former metal or wooden object that supports the work being shaped. A former can be used to ensure that all the units in a project are identical.

fusing joining metals using heat but without solder. A range of surface effects can be created using this technique, by varying the amount of heat applied to different areas.

jig device used for holding or forming work, particularly where several identical items are to be made.

jump ring small ring used as a connection between links in a chain or between a pendant and a chain or cord.

liver of sulphur (potassium sulphide) oxidising agent used to colour silver and other metals.

malleable capable of being beaten or rolled into thin sheets. Most non-ferrous metals are malleable, gold being the most malleable.

mallet tool used to shape metal without causing damage to its surface. A silversmith uses a rolled hide mallet, which is heavier than a wooden one.

mandrel tapered steel rod, usually round, sometimes oval, square or other shapes. Also called a *triblet*.

needle files small files, usually sold in sets, that are used in awkward places that cannot be reached by full-sized files.

pallion tiny piece of solder that is placed over the join to be soldered.

pickle solution of sulphuric acid that is used to dissolve spent flux from the surface of metal after soldering. The acid pickle is the only method by which spent flux can be removed.

planishing hammering metal with polished or textured hammers to create an attractive surface finish, and also to stretch the metal, when sizing rings, for example.

punch and die device for making holes in sheet metal using a shearing action. Sometimes called a disc cutter.

pusher short steel rod with a handle that fits in the palm of the hand, used for pushing the bezel on to a cabochon.

repoussé decorative finish applied to sheet metal using hammers and punches. The work is usually embedded in a block of pitch and worked from the reverse as well as the front, until a high relief is achieved. See *chasing*.

rolling mill device consisting of smooth steel rollers encased in a cast iron frame, used to reduce the thickness of metal. Textured material can be added between the rollers to transfer a pattern to the metal surface.

rouge very fine compound of red iron oxide that is used for polishing, and is applied last in the polishing process.

shears tool used for cutting sheet metal by shearing. Shears are rather like heavy duty scissors.

silver soldering joining metals using heat, a flux and an alloy containing silver.

stake polished metal former that is used as a support against which to hammer metal. Maintenance of stakes is important as any imperfections will be transferred to the work.

sterling silver an alloy of 92.5% silver and 7.5% copper, which is the most commonly used metal in jewellery making.

swaging forming metal by means of a shaped tool or a die, used with hammering or pressure to create the desired form.

toggle clasp A catch with a bar on one side that is pushed through a hole on the opposite side. The bar lies across the hole in slight tension, which prevents it from coming loose.

try square a tool used to check, or 'try', that an end is square to an edge and to scribe a line square to an edge.

Water of Ayr stone fine abrasive stone used with water to create a dead smooth surface prior to polishing. Water of Ayr stone can be shaped with files or emery cloth to reach into awkward corners.

work hardening any metal worked by bending, twisting, hammering or drawn becomes harder and more brittle. The metal will eventually break unless it is *annealed*.

Index